SUNDAY SAUCE

SUNDAY SAUCE

When Italian-Americans Cook

Daniel Bellino-Zwicke

Daniel Bellino-Zwicke

Sunday Sauce
Copyright 2013 by Daniel Bellino Zwicke.

For information email author at
 danielbellinozwicke@yahoo.com.

First Edition
First Edition Broadway Fifth Press 2013
New York, New York
Cover Design Daniel Bellino Zwicke
Cover photo property of Daniel Bellino Zwicke
First Published by Broadway Fifth Press 2013
New York, New York 10014

Library of Congress Cataloging-in-Publication Data,
Zwicke Bellino, Daniel
Sunday Sauce
ISBN- 10: 1490991026
ISBN- 13: 978-1490991023

1. Zwicke Bellino, Daniel, Cooks – New York(State)—New York—Nonfiction, I Title

Sunday Sauce

Daniel Bellino-Zwicke

Dedicated to

Lucia Bellino
Bazzy
Fran Bellino
Aunt Helen

Italian-American New Yorkers
&
Italian-Americans Everywhere

READ THIS FIRST

Dear Reader,

I "Thank You" for obtaining this book. It is my sincerest wish that you do enjoy it and that the book brings you joy and pleasure and gives you a nice insight into Italian-America, the Italian-American people their food, their eating habits and rituals of the table, how and what they eat, and the dishes they love. For this book is about people, their food, and love of food, love of people.

I do hope you enjoy the recipes and the little stories peppered with facts on the food, the origins, and factual as well as mythical points.

I'd like to note, that though this is a cookbook, it is *not set up in your normal cookbook formatting*. This being that most cookbooks start out with appetizers, which all good Italians know, is the Antipasto Course of Antipasto and Antipasti. Then you might have soups, followed by; fish, poultry, meat, and possibly sweets. And in the case with Italian cookbooks, you will have a section on "Pasta" (after the antipasti) or as many Italian-Americans still say "Maccheroni." This cookbook is a book of Italian-America's favorite dishes and featuring the most esteemed dish of all "Sunday Sauce," or as many call it, "Gravy," the famed dish of a million Italian-American Sunday Dinners. This book doesn't start with the Antipasto Course as most Italian cookbooks do, but with the centerpiece and title dish of the book *Sunday Sauce*, a.k.a. *Gravy*. Then you will have dishes that might be part of a Sunday Sauce or spin-off of Sunday Sauce as with our beloved Meatball Parm Sandwiches, Braciola, and Meatballs.

Like any cookbook, you do not have to and most likely won't read it cover-to-cover, but go to the table of con- tents and pick out a particular dish or subject and go to that page. That being said, this is a cookbook filled with many stories and facts of the dishes within, and this is one cookbook that can very will be read from beginning to end, cover-to-cover, for this book does tell a story, many in fact. So either way, you can read it, skipping here and there, or cover to cover. Just please enjoy, delve-in, read the stories, the recipes, cook the dishes, and again, "I Thank You."

Daniel

Daniel Bellino-Zwicke

CONTENTS

Sunday Sauce

CONTENTS

Daniel Bellino-Zwicke

Sunday Sauce

11

Daniel Bellino-Zwicke

12

Sunday Sauce

"Italian-Americans"

Italian-Americans, a breed apart, we have culture, rituals, traditions, our own style and language, especially in Brooklyn, Da Bronx, South Philly, and Jersey "Soprano Territory," as well as Boston's Italian neighborhood The East End. We love family, music, Pavorotti, Sinatra, Dino (Dean Martin), Frankie Valli, Jerry Vale and *"Al di La."* As part of our culture, we have an abundance of great music and recordings of such recording artists as Mario Lanza and Louie Prima. There are great writers like; Mario Puzo and Gay Talese, with Film Directors; Martin Scorsese of Raging Bull, Goodfellas, and Casino fame, a film Marty collaborated on with Italian-American writer Nick Peliggi, also from New York. There's also the great Francis Ford Coppola of Godfather and notable wine fame as well. And speaking of wine fame in America and The World and of Italian-Americans, let's not forget Robert Mondavi who almost single handily put American Wine on the map as concerns the prestige of American Wine from which it went from average to be among the greatest in the World.

Italian-America has had its share of great Boxers as well, in the form of the 2 Rocky's, Rocky Graziano and Rocky Marciano. There was Ray "Boom-Boom" Mancini, and The Raging Bull himself, Jake La Motta. And speaking of Rocky's, there was that Rocky Guy of Philadelphia, one Rocky Balboa "The Italian Stallion" created and played to beautiful perfection by an Italian Stallion from Hells Kitchen, New York, one Sylvester Stallone.

Ball-Players you ask? The Baseball Hall of Fame is filled with great Italian-American ball players like; Yogi Berra, Phil Rizzutto (The Holy Cannoli Guy), and the great "Joe D," The Yankee Clipper "Joltin Joe DiMaggio."

On the gridiron we had one of the Biggest & All Time Greatest in the spectrum of football, Vince Lombardi of Englewood New Jersey. So great that The Super Bowl Trophy is named after him.

Wow, a lot of these great Italian-Americans are from New York and New Jersey? How bout that? Who are they? The list is pretty long. Ready? Of course the list starts with the greatest and most beloved Italian-American of all, Frank. Yes, Frank Sinatra, a legend who is not but is close to being almost "God-Like," that's how esteemed, loved, admired, and respected this man was, and still is. Frank Sinatra is revered to the highest extent of reverence possible. Frank Sinatra born and bred in Hoboken, New Jersey, then buying his first home in Hasbrouk Heights, New Jersey, starting a family with his first wife Nancy who was from Lodi. All of Frank's 3 children, Frank Jr., Nancy, and Tina were all born in New Jersey before Frank moved out west to Hollywood, California before later settling in Palm Springs. But once a Jersey Boy "Always a Jersey Boy."

Gay Talese, Joe Pesci, Frederico Casteluccio, Frank Vincent, Connie Francis, Danny DeVito and Cousin Jack (half Italian), that's one John Jack Nicholson who was born in St. Vincents Hospital in

Greenwich Village, New York and grew up in Neptune, New Jersey near cousin (Cugino) Danny. So Jack is both a New Yorker and Jerseyite. Just like me. So you've also got John Travolta from Englewood Cliffs and Frankie Valli from Bellville, New Jersey.

Now, how bout the New Yorkers? The list is long; but I'll give you the short-list; Al Pacino (Da Bronx), Robert DeNiro, Martin Scorsese (Elizabeth Street), Dion Dimucci (Bronx), Tony Bennett, also known as Anthony Bennedetto from Astoria Queens, Jake LaMotta (Bronx), Rocky Grazianno of the Lower East Side, and-on-and-on.

So as we know the Italians love their music, Amore, nice clothes, rituals, this-that-and-every-other-thing. Yes, but thee greatest, most beloved and of greatest importance of all these things we love and do, there is nothing more important than "Food," after family and good health that is. Yes important as music is, and Amore, food is number one, and so you will see. Read on my friends.

MANGIA !
"When Italian-Americans Eat"

It wasn't so long ago, about twenty-five years, when the menus in most Italian restaurants in the United States looked pretty much all the same, almost Cookie-Cutter-Like. With few exceptions, most restaurants had pretty much a standardized menu that varied little from one restaurant to the next. They'd have menu items like the standard Cold Antipasto with Salami, Cheese, Olives, Provolone, and Roast Peppers. There'd be Baked Clams, or Clams Casino, Prosciutto and Melon, Shrimp Cocktail, Mozzarella and unripe out of season tomatoes, Manicotti, Lasagna, Ravioli, Spaghetti and Meatballs, the ubiquitous Chicken Parm and Veal Parmigiano, Veal Marsala, and Tortoni & Spumoni for dessert. Need I go on? You get the message, and if you're older than forty, you defiantly know what I mean. Then, about thirty years ago or so, some people started opening restaurants that were breaking that old Italian-American Red-Sauce Restaurant cookie cutter mold. Restaurants that were throwing out most if not all of the old cliché dishes of the past and replacing them with a multitude of pretty much authentic dishes from all regions of Italy.

Restaurateur's started taking things more seriously, and you started seeing things like Carpaccio, Rapini con Salsice, Parparadelle con Coniglio, and TiramiSu. These dishes that were the new thing twenty-five years ago, but have now become so popular that they too are now cliché as well, just as those of the previously old cliché dishes of yore (50's, 60's, 70's). The dishes that were new back in the mid to late 80s are now on the verge of becoming as out of vogue as Stuffed-Shells and Veal Parmigiano were way back when, but as they say, "history has a way of repeating itself," and those dishes like Veal Parm, Manicotti, and the old lot of dishes are staging a comeback, and in a big way at that. Why? Because those dishes that had become disdained by many were "guess what," great dishes in the first place. They were tasty then (That's why they became so Popular), "they are tasty now," and they always will be tasty. They're just Wonderful Classic Old-School Italian-American Red-Sauce dishes, "plain and simple," and because they are so tasty, and so wonderful, they eventually staged comebacks, thus the case with such popular dishes as Chicken and Veal Parmigiano, Manicotti, and Spaghetti with Meatballs. There was a point in time when these dishes became so popular that people got sick of them and looked down at them as cliché and of bad taste.

Not everyone looked down on these dishes back then, not Italian-Americans, but a good segment of the general population did. The people wanted something new. They did not realize that these dishes were forming a truly legitimate cuisine of their own, in Italian-American Cuisine. But with a turn toward the more authentically prepared Italian Food of Italy the old dishes of American Italian Red Sauce Restaurants lost favor with a significant percentage of people in New York and other parts of the country. The new, more authentic (authentic to Italy) Italian dishes were "In" and the old cliché dishes of Italian-America were *"Out."* The old cliché dishes started to disappear off menus, but in time the same people who had disdained them for some time, started missing them. People started getting nostalgic for the past and craving nice simple *comfort foods*, and dishes like Veal Parmgiano, Chicken Parmigiano, and Spaghetti with Meatballs and such. The old favorites that lost favor for a little while were missed. In time, these dishes started to reappear. They were revived through nostalgia and simply because they were so tasty and wonderful to begin with, no-matter that they became overly popular and scorned simply for being so popular in the first place. It was never that these dishes were not liked for their flavor, but the fact that because they were so appetizing, people wanted them and ordered them all the time, and for quite a number of years, some people just became tired of them, simply because they were so prevalent, they became common. Some might say "Overly-Popular." Shall we say, they became too popular for their own good, and this was the main reason that they lost favor. That and the fact that people were jumping on the Band-Wagon an they wanted to try all these new Italian dishes that were hitting the scene.

So many of the old-school dishes lost favor for 15 years or so. But people started missing them, the *Comfort Food* craze hit, and people were craving and asking for those temporarily disdained cliché old-school Italian Dishes of the past. Now these dishes were coined Comfort Food, food from our childhood. They became popular and much loved once again.

Places like Rocco's on Sullivan Street, Gino's on Lexington Ave., Lanza's in the East Village, Patsy's on 56th (Frank Sinatra's favorite restaurant), and a multitude of places down in Little Italy, in "Da Bronx," Brooklyn, and all across America are now busier than ever. Their popularity attributed to the wonderful, comforting old style cooking they serve, aged décor preserved, as well as the fact that they weren't influenced by the multitude of fleeting trends that came and went. These old-school Italian restaurants stood the test of time. They stayed old and true, charming, and traditional, "Thank God they did!"

In the past few years there has been a craze for So-Called "Comfort Food." Things like pork chops, mashed potatoes, Fried Chicken, and yes, Chicken Parmigiano, as well as Spaghetti & Meatballs, and Eggplant Parmigiano. These tasty old dishes have all come back in a very big way. I'm ecstatic to say how happy I am to see these restaurants so popular again, as they are literally part of our beloved Italian-American Heritage, New York City History, and American Cultural History as a whole.

Although I was happy in the 1980's when there was a great surge of all those new restaurant openings that served authentic Italian food, with a greater array of choices, I must now say that it gives me and a legion of others, much comfort that we still have a fair number of these old style, so-called "Red Sauce Restaurants" left today. They still stand, and are doing better than ever. We're lucky they were not all totally obliterated. "Dam Lucky!" There is even a growing movement of restaurateurs specifically going for and opening Old-School Type Red-Sauce Italian Restaurants with the two Frankie's of Frankie's Spuntino leading the way along with the so-called Torrisi Boys; Rich Torrisi and Mario Carbone of "Parm," Torrisi Italian Specialties, and *Carbone* fame leading the way.

Whenever I go out to eat at an Italian Restaurant in New Jersey with my family (all still in Jersey), I usually always order either Chicken or Veal Parmigiano. I never order any of the Specials that they try to get fancy with, but invariably these dishes are not very good, they never work (the non Italian Specials that is). Often someone in our crowd orders one of the *Specials* and is disappointed. The moral of the story is that when you're in one of those old style Italian restaurants, stick with what they do best, the tried and true Old-School Favorites like; Spaghetti & Meatballs, and or Chicken or Veal Parmigiano and the like. You know what I mean?

Many people will tell you that that Spaghetti and Meatballs or Veal Parmigiano are not Italian. Well Italians do eat Meatballs, but not with pasta. The Meatballs are served on their own with Tomato Sauce or with Polenta and sauce, and even mashed potatoes. "Yes Italians in Italy eat mashed potatoes." It was our Italian immigrant ancestors who first put the two together, Spaghetti and Meatballs that is!

Although I must say, that I feel that although it may not have been a known practice, that over time, there must have been quite a good number of Italians in Italy who over the years put maccheroni together with Meatballs on the same plate. "It would be utterly impossible that of the Billions of meals cooked in Italy over the years, that somewhere in homes in Sicily, Campania, Puglia, Calabria, or even Tuscany for that matter, that no Italian mothers or nonnas did not put Meatballs and Pasta on the same plate. "Impossible I tell you, utterly impossible for it not have happened! The odds are way against it!"

So, what I'm saying is that, although it was not documented, I'm sure that in some households in Italy over the years, there had to be families who cooked Meatballs in Sauce (Gravy), dressed the pasta, Spaghetti, Rigatoni, or Ziti with the Sauce, and threw a couple Meatballs on the same plate as well. I guarantee this happened. And if it did, that makes it Italian.

Yes, the Italian immigrants at the turn of the century (1900) were primarily a poor lot. Meat was a bit expensive, and any meal that might include it, might have to be stretched with much cheaper ingredients in order to feed the entire family. That cheaper ingredient was none other than, yes, you guessed it, *pasta*, a.k.a. *maccheroni;* spaghetti, ziti, rigatoni and such. I'm sure, some of these Italian ladies who came to America from Campania, Sicily, Calabria, Genoa, and Apulia, as a treat, would put one or two Meatballs on a plate with pasta, and on the same plate in order to have less work by washing less dishes. Thus the *invention* of Spaghetti & Meatballs, the Genesis so to speak? I hope you will understand that in the history of the World, food and cuisines are constantly changing. They do not ever stay exactly the same. There are always little changes here-and-there. If there wasn't, you would never have the great French Cuisine that we have today and have had for some time, if Catherine d'Medici did not bring her great Florentine Chefs from Italy when she married the King of France, whatever his name was. More important to many in the course of history is that she brought her great Florentine Chefs who helped spawn and change what in France was quite primitive and not very tasty food at the time. These Florentine Chefs started what is now French Cuisine with such dishes like Duck al 'Orange, Crepes, Béchamel, and scores of other dishes of which people think are French in origin but are not. They are Italian, "and guess what?" It was Italians who "created" French Cuisine and "taught" the French How to Cook. Basta la Pasta!

So you see cuisines and ethnic food changes over time. The instance I gave you of Italians teaching the French how to cook and creating French Cuisine is only one of many in the history of the World. Another instance that has been going on for a little over 100 years now is the creation of Italian-American Cuisine, a *legitimate cuisine* that is based mostly on the cuisine of the mother country Italy, but it does have its differences and own creations like; Veal Parm, Spaghetti & Meatballs, Chicken Parmigiano, the Muffuletta, and a few others.

Here's an interesting fact for you. Did you know that Meatballs are many times more popular in the United States than in Italy? The ratio is not even close. "True," Italians don't eat nearly as many Meatballs as do Italian-Americans, and all

Americans for that matter, everyone loves them. Yes, Meatballs are Italian and they are eaten occasionally, just not normally with Pasta, not that anyone will admit to anyway!

What "Spaghetti and Meatballs" happen to be, is a *great* Italian-American Classic, which is defiantly a cuisine of its own. The Meatballs have been made by scores of Italian-American "Mamma's" and Nonna's over the past 125 years or so. Meatballs, Polpette, the variations are many and Italian-American boys and men it seems love them much more than the girls do, and they love them best the way Mamma makes them.

Some people make them with just Beef, while others make them with a combination of beef, veal, and pork, and in Italy the most popular ones are made with veal. Some Mamma's put in a lot of garlic while others put just a little. The same goes for breadcrumbs. You can use either Pecorino or Parmigiano, or a combination of both. The two main objectives are that the Meatballs are soft and that they are *Tasty*. Make plenty of them and you can make a delicious Meatball Parmigiano Sandwich the next day, another great Italian-American Classic and something that I've never seen in Italy. Meatball Parm Sandwiches are great never the less.

One dish that has completely disappeared from Italian restaurant menus, are Stuffed Shells. They are large Seashell Shaped Pasta that are filled with Ricotta and Pecorino and baked with tomato sauce and a little Mozzarella Cheese on top. The ones my mother Lucia used to make were "The Best." They were one of our favorites when we were kids and I used to love when my mom would let me stuff a few of the shells with the ricotta myself. Then when all the shells were stuffed, I'd stick my finger in the Ricotta bowl and lick it, the same way you would do with the bowl of cake batter which I'd eat as well. "Know what I mean? Yummy!" Now that I think about it, I have not had any Stuffed Shells for quite some time now. Think I'll pick up a box of Ronzoni Shells one of these days and make some stuffed ones for the first time in ages. When I was a child, I didn't know that there were any other companies outside of Ronzoni that produced commercial pasta. And, although nowadays I always buy Italian Pasta made in Italy, there are two exceptions for me. When it comes to Pastina or Large Shells for Stuffing, "only Ronzoni will do."

When I was growing up back in the 60's and 70's, Ronzoni was by far the most popular Brand of Pasta. In fact, as a child, I don't know if I can remember any other, other than the *Prince* brand ,which was far less popular. They didn't have all the other imported and domestic ones back in the sixties.

My mother only used Ronzoni, and quite a lot of it, especially, Ziti, #9 Spaghetti, Fusilli, Ditalini, Pastina, and yes, large Shells for stuffing. "Ronzoni Sono Buoni", was their slogan. Meaning, "Ronzoni is so good." I used to use Ronzoni when I first started cooking because I grew up with it, and Ronzoni is a very good product. I stopped using Ronzoni a number of years ago because when I am making an Italian meal, I use as many Italian products as I can. I use Italian made Pasta, Olive Oil, Porcini Mushrooms, Tomatoes, anchovies, vinegar, capers, Prosciutto de Parma, and Parmigiano Reggiano.

The only times that I've bought Ronzoni over the past several years is when I get nostalgic for Pastina, and now when I make the stuffed-shells in the near future. Pastina is very tiny Star-Shaped egg pasta that Italian Mamma's make for their piccolo bambini (little children). When I was a very young boy, this was my absolute favorite. I would ask my Mom to make it for me all the time. She used to cook the Pastina and dress them in gobs of butter, and sprinkle Parmesan on top. "YUM yum yum!!!" I used to go crazy for my Pastina. "I still do!"

Note: After I wrote this chapter, I ran into my friend Antoinetta who was born and grew up near Naples, Italy. I asked her if she or other Italians ever ate Meatballs and pasta on the same plate. Antoinetta said yes, sometimes they did, though not with spaghetti, but usually a short maccheroni like rigatoni or cavatelli. You, see? It's now confirmed. Basta!

SUNDAY

Sunday! In the Italian-American household this is thee most important day of the week, for Sunday is the day the whole family gets together; Mama, Papa, Nonna, Nonno (Grandma and Grandpa), brother and sister, Aunts and Uncles, cousins (Cujino) and a few close family friends may stop by as well. They'll sit around the table, and if they're like my family (The Bellino's) they'll eat all day long.

Yes for Italian-Americans, Sunday is the most important day of the week. The day the whole family gets together for the all important Sunday Meal, which most likely will be a Sunday Sauce (Gravy) made by one or a group effort of several women and maybe a man or two. Well the "*Sauce*," a.k.a. Gravy, the Sunday Sauce can be made by several ways, but it's sot often one particular way is most popular. In our family, it might be Aunt Helen or Aunt Fran making the *Sauce*. Uncle Tony is a great cook too, but he would make the roast when we had them, either; Pork, Veal, Lamb, or Beef.

Quite often the Sunday meals at our house might very well be the beloved Sunday Sauce. We'd have the Sunday Sauce about a third of the time. Sometimes my Aunts would lay out an Antipasto Platter of Salami, with Provolone, Roast Red Peppers, Celery, and Sicilian Olives. This antipasto is ubiquitous to the Italian-American enclave, especially when in an Old-School Red Sauce Italian Restaurant. The antipasto may vary on this base antipasto Italian-American Classic. It could be made with Giardiniera Salad of pickled carrots, cauliflower, and peppers, along with Salami, Olives, and Provolone. Most times Provolone is on the platter, or fresh Mozzarella or both. We'd sometimes have an antipasto of Caponata, fresh tomatoes, and olives, or we might more simply have a tossed salad of lettuce (usually Iceberg) with cucumbers, and tomato slices. The salad would precede the main or pasta course if there was a separate pasta course, usually when we had home-made Ravioli.

Sunday is the day for Sunday Sauce, but this doesn't mean that every Sunday you ate Sunday Sauce (Gravy). The most important thing about the Sunday meal was the simple fact that everyone was getting together to see each other sharing a meal and each others company, spending time with loved-ones. Sometimes Uncle Tony would make one of his famous roasts; Beef, Veal, Lamb, or Pork, or one of my favorites from uncle Tony, his wonderful version of Veal Marsala, an Italian-American Classic, and more specifically a Sicilian-American favorite, as Marsala Wine that is the base of the sauce comes from Marsala, Sicily and my good friends the Rallo family are renowned for theirs. Anyway, my Uncle Tony's Veal Marsala is the "Best" I've ever tasted anywhere, "Basta."

So, as I've said, Sunday is the day you most often eat Sunday Sauce, but this doesn't mean that you eat it every Sunday or that you couldn't make one on a Wednesday, or any day of the week, Sunday Sauce is always good. And all this being said, though of course we ate and enjoyed different dishes like Uncle Tony's Veal Marsala, a Roast Pork or whatever. The Sunday Sauce (Gravy with Sausage, Braciole, & Meatballs) was without question the favorite and most craved dish of all, and for many reasons; the Meatballs, the Sausages, and Braciole and the fact that you could make a Meatball Parm on Monday if any of these precious little treasures were leftover.

In our house we might start with a traditional antipasto or a mixed green salad, then one of Uncle Tony's roasts, Aunt Fran's famed Eggplant Parmigiano, or Aunt Helen's Chicken Cacctiatore.

A Sunday meal with the Bellino Family was usually an all day affair. We'd start with some sort of antipasto, move on to the main and yes the beloved Sunday Sauce with Sausage, Meatballs, and Beef Braciola were always welcome. After the main course was cleared away and everyone had some time to rest and digest, the very important course of coffee and desert (Dolci) would be served. This course would take up the bulk of the day and meal, as once my aunts and uncles gathered round the table for dessert and coffee with a little Anisette, they'd sit there relaxed and get into some spirited chats of all sorts of things; family matters, friends, sports, gossip, politics, local and world news. And they'd sit around the table for hours. We kids mainly wanted to get a bit of all the different cookies, cakes, and pastries that my aunts made and sometimes it was all homemade cakes and cookies from the aunts or a combination of desserts made by family members and embellished with some Cannoli and

Sfogliatelle from Sorrento's Bakery on Main Street in Lodi.

The gown-ups would literally sit around the table for three to four hours or more: chatting, sipping on espresso or American Coffee, nibbling on a cookie or some Anisette Toast here and there and just talk and talk and talk about *this-that-everything* and anything. Every once and a while a card game might break out amongst the men, especially when my Uncle Frank Pinto was still alive. The woman would break off separately still chatting and sipping coffee and the children would usually break off as well, into two or three separate groups of older and younger cousins, boys and girls.

Even as a child, I always loved listening to my aunts and uncles telling stories chatting about this and that, and I'd listen for a while then break-off into one of the kids groups down in the cellar or playing outside, but we'd all keep periodically keep going back to the kitchen table to see the elders, get some more sweets, and catch a bit of the chatter. "Ah the good Old Days." And once I grew up, gathering round the table with Aunts, Uncles, Cousins, brothers, and sister; eating, drinking, and talking about everything and anything became one of the most special and precious things of my entire life, The Table, "La Tavola," La Famiglia.

SUNDAY SAUCE

Of all the fine traditions of the Italian-American enclave in the United State, the Sunday afternoon ritual of making and eating a Sunday Sauce, a.k.a. "*Gravy*" is Italian-America's most *Time-Honored* of all. Mamma, Grandma (Nonna), whoever will make their celebrated "Sunday Sauce" and all is glorious. Sunday Sauce? What is it? Well, first off, Sunday Sauce, or as many of us call it, *Gravy* or simply *"Sauce,"* is without question thee number-1 undisputed "Supreme Dish" of our great Italian-American Cuisine and the Italian-American community as a whole. "It doesn't get any better than gather with family and making a Sunday Sauce on Sunday" Ok, now, to be more specific for those who may not know about Sunday Sauce (Gravy), there are a number of variations on the theme. Most Sunday Sauces are made with Italian Sausages, Braciole, and Meatballs. Some people make their versions with; Beef or Pork Neck, while others make their Gravy (Sunday Sauce) with just Sausage and Meatballs, like Pete Clemenza in Francis Ford Coppola's great movie, The Godfather. The most popular version is with Sausages, Meatballs, and Braciole. Some may throw in Chicken Thighs or a Veal Shank into this mix. A Sunday Sauces can be made with any combination of these aforementioned meats. The meats are slowly simmered for several hours in a "Sauce" made with tomatoes, minced onions, and garlic. I generally like to make my

Sunday Sauce *Gravy* with; Sausages, Meatballs, and Pork Ribs. Other times I'll make it with Sausage, Meatballs, and Braciole.

An old tradition in some families is that mother or Grandma would start the *Sauce* early on a Sunday morning, get all the ingredients in the pot and start the *Gravy* simmering away for an hour or so on top of the stove. She'll then put it in the oven for a couple hours while everyone goes to Church. When you get back home, the Sauce will be ready. "Ready to be devoured that is!"

Our family would usually start our Sunday meal with the most traditional Italian-American-Antipasto of roast peppers, Salami, Olives, Celery, and Provolone. After that, it's on to the *Main Event* of Maccheroni and Sunday Sauce, a dish which is something so Blissfully and Pleasurably Sublime, that it is almost "Sinful." Oh, *yes* it is.

When a meal centered around a Sunday Sauce is announced, one can have visions of *Blissful Ecstasy* at thoughts of eating Pasta laden with Italian Sausages, Savory Meatballs, Beef Braciola, and succulent Pork Ribs. All this has been slowly simmered to culinary perfection. Yes just the thoughts can enrapture one into a *delightful frenzy* of the "Most Blissful Feelings" of smelling, seeing, and consuming all the ingredients; the Sausages, Meatballs, the Gravy. Yes a Sunday Sauce can and does have such effects on one's mind, body, and soul. And, I do not want to sound prejudice, but this is pure fact, it is the Male of the Italian-American species who Love The Sunday Sauce in all its form, far more than the female sex. True! Meatballs too!

And Italian-American men and boys Love and hold oh-so-dear, their Meatballs, Sunday Sauce, Sausage & Peppers, and Meatball Parm Sandwiches as well.

The Sunday Sauce that my mother would make was with Meatballs and Beef Braciole. My memories are vivid watching my mother stuffing the Braciole with garlic, parsley, Pecorino Romano, and Pignoli Nuts, then tying the bundles with butchers cord to hold the Braciole together as they slowly simmered in the Gravy. Another fond memory was helping my mother roll and shape the Meatballs.

As for me, my Sunday Sauce can vary depending on my mood. One thing I Love to do when making my sauce is to add Pork Spareribs to the Gravy. *Gravy* by the way is what many people in the New York, New Jersey (Soprano Territory) area call Sunday Sauce, particularly in Brooklyn. Not many people make their Sunday Sauce with the Pork Ribs, but to me they are phenomenal, and anyone who tries them, they are immediately hooked. As I think back, none of the ladies in our family put Pork Spare Ribs into their Gravy. I guess I read or heard about some people doing it, and I believe it was about 15 years ago or so that I started adding the Ribs into my *Sauce*. I haven't looked back ever since. I Love them, as does everyone whom I serve them to, and when I make a Sauce, these babies go fast. The ribs that is.

Yes, whenever I make my sauce with Pork Ribs, my friends go nuts for them, and most are surprised, as they might never have had Ribs in a Sunday Sauce before. They didn't know that you could use Pork Spareribs.

The ribs are traditional with some but not all. It is quite a shame for those who don't add the ribs as they give the sauce a quite wonderful flavor, and the Ribs themselves, "Yumm." The Ribs that simmer long and slow become quite tender, and they literally "Melt-in-Your-Mouth."

Whenever I make the *Sauce*, and I'm dishing it out to friends and family, I always make sure that I have my fare share of the Ribs. Pork Ribs cooked in this manner, simmering in the sauce are oh so succulent and tasty, they are Beyond-Belief-Tasty. These Sunday Sauce Ribs are literally "Out-of-this-World." And what to serve with the Sunday Sauce you ask? Any short Maccheroni such as Rigatoni, Ziti, or Cavatelli are best.

The rituals of cooking, serving, and eating Sunday Sauce is a time honored one. It is a quite a beautiful thing, same as making a Mole in Mexico, Cassoulet in France or Paella in Spain. They are all wonderful things of beauty that delight mans every sensory perception; sight, smell, taste, and feel. First, you probably smell the Sauce's heady aroma wafting through the air. The smell is so intoxicating; it gets your juices flowing immediately. Once you smell it, you want it, and can't wait to sink you teeth into it. Second you will see it in all its gloriousness. You will then eat, whereupon you taste and feel and experience one of Italian-America's greatest pleasures, the Sunday Sauce Italian Gravy. A Sunday Sauce (Gravy) takes time and effort to make. It is made and served with Love. All these great dishes bring together friends and family, and for Italian-Americans, Sunday Sauce is King of all dishes.

If you utter the term Sunday Sauce or "Gravy" to any number of millions of Italian-Americans, they will immediately start salivating at the simple mention of its name. The wheels start turning in their heads, with thoughts of how tasty it is, with its various components; the Meatballs, Sausages, Braciole, maybe Ribs, Beef Neck, or Pig Skin Braciole (Coteca), as well as the Pasta, and the Gravy itself. They think about sitting at the table with friends, family, people they love. They'll ponder the Antipasti, wondering what it might be; mixed Salumi, Baked Clams, Grilled Calamari? And with the meal, there will surely be Wine. Italian Wine, which might be a good Chianti, or perhaps Montepulciano d'Abruzzo. With Uncle Frank and Uncle Tony, the wine was usually Carlo Rossi Paisano or Gallo Hearty Burgundy, two solid Italian-American Winemakers.

When thinking of a Sunday Sauce, you'll think about the warmth in the air, of loved ones, Sinatra, Dino, and the Sunday Sauce itself. "It's a beautiful thing!" If you've never done it, "Try it!" If you haven't cooked one for some time, plan a get-together with friends and family, soon. Sunday Sauce, It brings people together, in a most *delightful* way. And as the Big Boys would say, "It's a Beautiful Thing."

SUNDAY SAUCE
(a.k.a. GRAVY)

This Sunday Sauce (Gravy) is the most popular version. It's made with; Sausage, Meatballs, and Braciole. Some, like Clemenza, make it with just Sausage & Meatballs. You can, as you'll see, add; Pork Ribs, Veal Shank, and various other items according to how you like it. This is a great one, sure you'll agree.

Ingredients:

½ cup olive oil
2 medium onions, minced
12 cloves garlic, minced
6 - 28 oz. cans of crushed tomatoes
1 small can tomato paste (optional)
2 lbs. sweet Italian sausage
1 cup water (don't worry, the water will evaporate by the time the sauce is done. You need it.)
1 teaspoon crushed red pepper
1 ½ teaspoons Sea Salt, 1 tablespoon black pepper
1 batch Braciole from recipe, page 62
1 batch of Meatballs from recipe on page 44

Preparation:

1. Place onions in olive oil in a large pot. Sauté onions over a low flame for 4 minutes. Add garlic and sauté on low flame with onions for 3 minutes.

2. Add all the tomatoes and water. Raise flame to high. Bring the tomatoes up to the boil, then lower the sauce to a very low simmer.

3. Season all the Braciole with salt & pepper. Brown the Braciole in a separate pan over medium to high heat until all the Braciole are nicely browned, about 10 minutes.

4. Place Braciole in pot with tomatoes and simmer over very low heat for 1 hour & 45 minutes.

5. In the same pan you browned the Braciole in, brown the sausages over medium heat until nicely browned, about 10 minutes. Add sausages to pot with tomatoes and the Braciole and cook over low heat for 30 minutes.

6. Make the Meatballs (recipe follows) up to the point where they have cooked in the oven for 10 minutes.

7. After the sausages have been cooking for 30 minutes, add the browned meatballs and cook over low heat for about 35 minutes, being careful not to break meatballs when you stir.

8. The Sauce (Gravy) is done. Total cooking time between 2 ½ and 3 hours.

9. Serve the sauce with your favorite Short Pasta such as Rigatoni, Cavatelli, Ziti, or whatever you like best.

"Now it's time to Mangia Bene. Enjoy!"

MEATBALLS

Spaghetti and Meatballs! What's more Italian than that? Well, a lot of things actually. There is a constant ongoing debate over whether "Spaghetti and Meatballs" is an authentic Italian dish or not. Of course spaghetti is very Italian and so are Meatballs, however Italians (in Italy) do not eat them together on the same plate. This is an Italian-American tradition and a great one at that, as Lidia Bastianich and others have written, Italian-American is a great cuisine in itself. The Cuisine of Italian-America is most truly authentic Italian with a few twists here and there, like eating Meatballs on the same plate with Spaghetti instead of two separate courses as they do in Italy. What's wrong with that? Maybe the Italian-American mammas of way back (100 years ago, around 1905) didn't want to clean twice as many dishes so they combined the two courses into one. This is quite plausible, and most certainly true. Even more plausible, and most likely the true reason that Spaghetti & Meatballs came into being was probably from poverty. These poor Italian families living on the Lower East Side of Manhattan, Brooklyn, Jersey, wherever, did not have much money, they had to stretch a buck as far as it would go. Some would have meat just once or twice a week at most. And when they could get their hands on some meat, ground meat was the cheapest. They'd make Meatballs with it, stretching them out with bread. And to further stretch the small amount of meat amongst the whole family, they'd serve these tasty little meatballs with Spaghetti. What better way to do so? A great idea don't you think? This is the Genesis of our beloved Italian-American dish of Spaghetti & Meatballs. Bravo to the Italian Mommas who first invented it, we all owe you a great debt of gratitude. "Mille Grazie," a *1,000 Thanks*.

Let me tell you one thing, in case you didn't know. Meatballs, and yes they are Italian and eaten in Italy, meatballs are infinitely more popular in the United States than they are in the mother country of Italy. Italian-Americans eat millions more of them a year than their Italian brethren. The Neapolitans and Sicilians eat them the most in Italy and because of the fact that these are the areas where the greatest number of Italian immigrants to the U.S. came from, this is the reason the dish became such a great favorite of Italian expatriates, their children, grandchildren, and millions of Americans, including people of other ethnic origins who happen to love Italian-American food. It is one of the world's great cuisines. You don't have to be Italian to love their food, the same as many Italian-Americans love to eat Chinese food. It's tasty, so we Mangia!!!

Oh yes, you want to know what kind of meat goes into the Meatballs? Well the most common in Italian America are Meatballs made with a mixture of; ground Beef, Pork, and Veal. However, many make their meatballs solely with Beef, and in Italy and especially Tuscany, Veal Meatballs, *Polpettini* are quite popular. Whatever meat you choose, just make the meatballs tasty, and you'll have people coming back for second, even third helpings.

One more thing, Meatballs in Sauce (Gravy) are great but if you ever want a little change when making them, I have another way that's quite tasty, I think you'll agree. When making Meatballs for a Sunday Sauce or to serve with Spaghetti on their own, reserve 8 or so meatballs that you don't cook in sauce. Brown these Meatballs, then pop in the oven to finish cooking and serve on their own without tomato sauce gravy, and just a little bit of the juices the Meatballs cook in, with some chopped fresh parsley on top. They taste great this way. You can serve as starter course (Antipasto), in a Sandwich, or as a main course with Mashed Potatoes, or a salad on the side or whatever you choose to serve them with, they're oh-so tasty when you make them this way, try them some time, your sure to agree.

MEATBALL RECIPE:

Ingredients:

1 lb. ground Beef
½ lb. ground Veal
½ Pound Ground Pork
4 tablespoons fresh Italian Parsley, chopped
1 minced onion
2 cloves garlic, minced
4 Tablespoons plain breadcrumbs
2 large eggs, ¼ cup Milk
Salt & pepper
½ cup grated Parmigiano or Pecorino

Note: If you want, instead of this beef, pork, and veal mixture, you can use just use Beef (2 lbs.) or 1 lb. Ground Beef & 1 lb. Veal.

PREPARATION:

1. In a small bowl, break and beat eggs. Add breadcrumbs and milk and let soak for 10 minutes.

2. In a large bowl, add all the remaining ingredients. Add eggs and mix well with your hands.

3. Shape meat mixture to from balls that are about 2 inches in diameter.

4. Coat the bottom of a cookie sheet or roasting pan with a thin film of olive oil. Cook Meatballs at 350 degrees for 10 minutes.

5. Take meatballs out of oven and simmer for 45 at low heat in a batch of Tomato Sauce from the tomato sauce recipe.

6. Serve Meatballs with Spaghetti for the Classic Italian American favorite Spaghetti and Meatballs or do as the Italians do, especially the Neapolitans and serve the sauce first with Spaghetti, Rigatoni, or ziti. Then serve the Meatballs as the main course with a Salad or potatoes on the side.

Daniel Bellino-Zwicke

SPAGHETTI & MEATBALLS

Spaghetti and Meatballs? What's more Italian than that? Well, it's Italian, "Italian-America" that is, and quite possibly the most famous dish of all. Famous for Italian-America and America itself. The dish is quite American, as the whole of America, of all ethnic backgrounds; Poles, the Irish, Jews, and Germans, Americans, they all eat and love this dish, called Spaghetti & Meatballs. Some make it good, others? Well we won't even go there. But no one makes Spaghetti & Meatballs like Italians, *Italian-Americans* that is! It's all about the Meatballs and the "Sauce" they cook in. Mamma, Grandma, Aunt Helen, they make the *best*, yes no one makes Meatballs like your Momma, Nonna, or one of your favorite aunts, yours and mine. That's the way it is with Italians. My Aunt Helen's was phenomenal!

Spaghetti & Meatballs is the favorite dish of many. Or maybe it's Lasagna, Spaghetti Vongole, and of course there's the most-supreme Italian-American dish of all, Sunday Sauce, or as some us call it, Gravy. No matter which is your favorite, Spaghetti & Meatballs is either at the top of the list, and if not the top, then way up there anyway.

To make Spaghetti & Meatballs, just use the previous recipe, cook a pound of imported Italian Spaghetti (or Ronzoni) for 3 to 4 people. Drain the spaghetti, put it back in the pot it cooked in, add a bit of olive oil and some of the "Sauce" that the Meatballs cooked in, divide the Spaghetti among 3 or 4 plates, put 2 to 4 meatballs on each plate and add some more Sauce.

Serve each person their own plate of Spaghetti and Meatballs, pass around some grated Pecorino Romano or Parmigiano Reggiano Cheese and enjoy. Cause when you have a tasty home-cooked plate of Spaghetti & Meatballs in front of you, all is fine in your World. Mangia Bene!

"Everything You See, I owe to Spaghetti!"

Sophia Loren

SINATRA

It's almost impossible to speak of Italian-America and Italian-American Food without mentioning Italian-America's favorite son and most cherished icon of all, one Francis Albert Sinatra, Frank Sinatra, or simply *Frank*. Frank Sinatra achieved great success in his life, becoming one of the 20th Century's Greatest Recording Stars, and a Movie Star, and Italian-American Icon as well. He achieved the great American Dream. Well, Frank went way beyond that. Most Italian Americans back then, the poor and middle class had upbringings like the Sinatra's (lower Middle-Class), whose greatest wish was to have a good job and possibly buy ones own home. That was the dream. Frank achieved it, but he had even greater dreams and high aspirations. Dreams of becoming a great and famous recording artist, which he achieved and far surpassed, not only to become one of the top musical artist of his day, but one of the greatest of the century and of *all-time*.

And as great as all these achievements were and still are, Frank was much more than that. Frank Sinatra was greatly beloved by his Italian-American brethren in an enormous way. He was and still is "almost *God-Like*" to his millions of loving and adoring fans. Frank Sinatra was a man who Italian-Americans looked up to, and bragged about as being one of our own, "Our Paesan." And not only to us (Italian-Americans), but to Americans of all creeds and races, who simply loved and enjoyed the beautiful music the man made.

Frank Sinatra couldn't read music, and in the beginning didn't have much musical training, but his voice, "The Voice" as Sinatra was known, his voice was his *instrument* and many great musicians who were classically trained and accomplished musicians often stated that Sinatra was a great musician, one of the greatest. For Frank, his wonderful voice was an instrument; an instrument Frank knew how to use to *absolute perfection*. The man could sing a love song and particularly a Torch Song like *no other*. Sinatra was the King of Torch Songs. One of the reasons many have said he was so adept at singing these torch songs, songs of *lost love*, was that when singing them, Frank was always singing about the *greatest love of his life*, Ava Gardner and the love lost between them.

Anyway, yes Frank's music was and still is some of the most wonderful of all time. People love and listen to the music, the music of Frank Sinatra. It makes them feel good, and brings back memories of good times, happy times, and even *bittersweet* feelings of *love lost*. The music of Frank Sinatra always moves you. I know it does for me. Bravo Frank, "*We Salute You*," your memory and music live on, today, tomorrow and forever more, we shall cherish and enjoy the music and the man, of one Francis Albert Sinatra, simply *Frank*.

FRANK'S WAY
Spaghetti & Meatballs

This is said to be the long lost recipe of Dolly Sinatra's Spaghetti & Meatballs that she would make for young Frankie back in Hoboken, New Jersey. Frankie loved these meatballs dearly. Dolly Sinatra was a locally renowned cook who loved cooking for her beloved son Frank. Not only did she cook for Frank and husband Marty, but for the famed Band Leader Tommy Dorsey and his band. When Frank's Star was just beginning to rise and he was singing with Tommy Dorsey's Band, Frank would often invite Tommy and other band members over to his parent's house in Hoboken, New Jersey. Dolly would feed the boys Spaghetti & Meatballs, Stuffed Artichokes, Eggplant Parmigiano, and other Sinatra Family favorites.

There is a funny passage in Kitty Kelley's book on Frank Sinatra, "His Way," when Dorsey and The Band are over the Sinatra household and Dolly is cooking for them. When dinner is ready, Dolly who is in the kitchen shouts out to Tommy and The Boys who are in the parlor, "Get in here you Bastards, I just made some Linguine." Pretty funny huh?

Make Dolly's Spaghetti & Meatballs, put on some Sinatra records, and you all will have the most wonderful dinner imaginable. That's the Gods honest truth.

Meatballs alla Sinatra Style

1 pound Ground Beef
1 pound Ground Pork
2 cloves Garlic, minced fine
2 Eggs
½ cup freshly grated Pecorino Romano Cheese
1/4 chopped Italian Flat Leaf Parsley
Salt and Black Pepper to taste
1 cup stale Italian bread, crumbled
1 cup of Milk or Water to soak stale bread in
olive oil for cooking

1. Mix all ingredients except olive oil in a large bowl.

2. Shape Meatballs into whatever size you prefer; small medium or large.

3. Fry Meatballs in olive oil over a medium heat until they are nicely browned.

4. Finish cooking in *Sauce (recipe follows).*

The SAUCE *"Dolly Sinatra's"*

1/4 Olive Oil
1 Large Onion chopped fine
3 Garlic cloves, peeled and chopped fine
5-28 oz. cans Tomatoes (crush 4 cans of tomatoes and leave 1 can of tomatoes whole) Use all the watery juice in sauce. Do not throw away
3 Tablespoons Tomato Paste
1 teaspoon Oregano
1 teaspoon Dry Basil
half glass of Red Wine (3 oz.)
1 teaspoon Sugar
Salt and Pepper to taste

1. Place olive oil and onions in a large pot. Turn heat on to medium, cook for 3 minutes. Lower heat to low, cook for 3 minutes.

2. Add chopped Garlic. Cook over low heat for 4 minutes.

3. Drain 1 can of whole tomatoes that you do not chop. Add whole tomatoes to pot, reserving the watery juice, which you add after all tomatoes have been added. Turn heat up to high and cook tomatoes. Break up tomatoes with wooden spoon. Cook tomatoes on high heat for 3-4 minutes.

4. Add wine. Cook over high heat for 4 minutes.

5. Add all remaining ingredients. Cook over high heat until sauce starts bubbling. Lower heat to very

low and cook over low heat for 1 hour.

7. After the sauce has been cooking for a half hour, start making the Meatballs.

8. Once the Meatballs have been shaped and browned, add the browned Meatballs into the Tomato Sauce that has been cooking for 1 hour.

9. Continue cooking the Sauce over low heat with the Meatballs for about 35 minutes.

10. Cook one pound of Spaghetti, Ronzoni or Imported Spaghetti from Italy. Figure on 1 pound for every 3 or 4 people. Use 1 pound for 3 people if you have hungry eaters who want seconds. Cook Spaghetti according to directions on package. Make sure the water is seasoned with salt and always at a rapid boil or it will become gummy.

11. When Spaghetti is finished cooking, drain in a colander, reserving about ¼ cup of the pasta cooking water. Add the drained Spaghetti back into the pot it cooked in. Add some of the "Sauce" to the Spaghetti and mix. Sprinkle a little Olive Oil over the Spaghetti and mix again.

12. Portion out Spaghetti onto plates or pasta bowls. Top the Spaghetti with some more Sauce. Add 2 or three Meatballs to each plate and serve to your guests.

SUNDAY GRAVY alla SINATRA

As a boy and young man, Dolly Sinatra would often make Frankie Spaghetti & Meatballs, which Frank loved all his life, from his Mom and at his favorite restaurant "Patsy's" on West 56th Street in New York.

Frank also liked Maccheroni with Sausage & Meatballs, otherwise known as Sunday Sauce or simply "Gravy" with Sausage & Meatballs.

MAKING SUNDAY GRAVY alla SINATRA

To make "Sunday Gravy alla Sinatra," simply make the above recipe for Spaghetti & Meatballs. Cook and brown 1 ½ pounds of Italian Sweet Sausages, and after you have completed step # 5 in previous recipe, add the browned Sausages and continue cooking and following the above recipe. After you have simmered the tomatoes and sausages for 1 - 1/4 hours, you will brown the meatballs and add to "Sauce." Continue cooking another 35 minutes, on the lowest simmer, and "Voila," you'll end up with Sunday Sauce Gravy alla Sinatra, "Just the way Frank liked it!"

PS .. For the most authentic version of the way Frank ate Sunday Sauce Gravy, use Ronzoni brand Spaghetti or Rigatoni pasta, and don't forget to have some Frank Sinatra records playing as you make the Meatballs & Gravy and when you are eating as well.

MUSIC to MAKE SUNDAY SAUCE By

Music to cook Sunday Sauce by? It's a great idea, and one that comes naturally. We've always done it.

When cooking Sunday Sauce or any Italian dishes, it always helps to have some great Italian background music. It doesn't hurt and only heightens an already wonderful experience, especially when you are entertaining guests.

There are two or three greats that always come to mind first. These prodigious Italian-American singers are of course, first; Frank Sinatra, then Dean "Dino" Martin (Crochetti), and Mr. Tony Bennett (Benedetto). They are the most famous, and for good reason, they are all just that, "Great." When it comes to overall artist, it's fare to say that Sinatra is usually at the top of the heap. But when it comes to actual Italian Songs, Dino, Jerry Vale, and Louie Prima have the *great one* beat for those particular types of songs. But hey, there's no way anyone can beat The Chairman of The Board, Mr. Francis Albert Sinatra. Dino is wonderful with his famed renditions of Volare and Amore, and you can't count out Jerry Vale with one of the most iconic and beloved to Italian Americans, especially in New York, with Jerry doing *Al di La*. Actually, many would say it is between Volare and Amore that are thee two most loved and popular Italian American songs. But no, for really true, hardcore Italians, and as I've already said, especially in New York, it is *Al Di La* that we truly love most. It is played at every Italian Wedding, bar none. Many artists have sung it, but it is Jerry Vale's that is most popular. Connie Francis's rendition is quite beautiful and best of the female singers, Connie being an Italian Girl from Jersey, real name Concetta Rosa Maria Franconero. "Now That's Italian!" Yes a lot of these great Italian-American artist changed their names back then, like Tony Bennett, real name Anthony Benedetto from Astoria Queens, New York and Dean Martin from Stubenville, Ohio, his real name was Dino Crochetti.

Back to Al Di La. If you've never heard the song, and I know there are many who haven't especially among the younger generation, do yourself a favor, and get a copy of Connie Francis or Jerry Vale singing this gorgeous song. Get both!

The song *That's Amore* is perhaps the most popular of all Italian-American songs for the general public. It is one of Dean Martin's signature songs and with the popularity of the movie Moonstruck, starring Cher, Nicholas Cage, and Danny Aiello, this song became even more famous. Louie Prima had great success with this song, and his tune "Angelina" The Waitress at The Pizzeria is a must listen to song of Italian-America and eating.

So we have lots of great Italian Songs and Italian American and Italian artists, but one stands alone at the top. Yes, you know who? He's A # 1, the one-and-only, *Frank Sinatra*.

A little PS. I almost forgot. The great Italian singer Andrea Bocelli from Tuscany. He sings beautiful Italian songs and has become quite popular, for good reason, he makes beautiful music.

Daniel Bellino-Zwicke

Al Di La

(Italian Lyrics)

Non credevo possibile,
Se potessero dire queste parole:
Al di là del bene più prezioso, ci sei tu.
Al di là del sogno più ambizioso, ci sei tu.
Al di là delle cose più belle.
Al di là delle stelle, ci sei tu.
Al di là, ci sei tu per me, per me, soltanto per me.
Al di là del mare più profondo, ci sei tu.
Al di là dei limiti del mondo, ci sei tu.
Al di là della volta infinita, al di là della vita.
Ci sei tu, al di la, ci sei tu per me.

Al Di La
(English)

I did not believe
I could ever say these words:
Beyond the most precious, that's where you are.
Beyond the most ambitious, that's where you are.
Beyond the most beautiful,
Beyond the stars, that's where you are.
Beyond everything, that's where you are for me, for
me, just for me.
Beyond the deepest sea, that's where you are.
Beyond the limits of the world, that's where you are.
Beyond infinite time, beyond life.
That's where you are, beyond everything, that's
where you are for me."

BRACIOLA

Of any of the dishes I remember my mother Lucia Bellino making most when I was a boy, they are; Stuffed Artichokes, Eggplant Parmigiano, Meatballs, Stuffed Peppers, Braciola, and Sunday Sauce. My mother's Sunday Sauce was made with Braciole and Meatballs and to this very day, I can still see my mother mixing the ground Beef, Pork and Veal with the eggs, cheese, garlic, and parsley, then rolling the meat mixture into meatballs one-by-one, ready to go into the Sunday Gravy at hand.

And of course I can never forget my mother seasoning the Braciole, rolling them and then tying them with string (I use toothpicks).

Braciola is a mainstay of the Italian-American Kitchen. It's loved by all, and not far behind Meatballs and Sausages as an Italian-American favorite. The recipe follows. You can make Braciola on it's own or as part of a Sunday Sauce with Meatballs and Sausages. You can make Braciole with Beef or Pork, and something you can also do something that not many do, is cook the Braciola without "Sauce." You slow-roast them, or even grill them. Try it sometimes; they're real tasty this way. Make the Braciole either way, they're always tasty as can be

BRACIOLA RECIPE

1 - 1/2 pounds Beef Flank Steak (cut the beef on an angle in pieces approximately 3 ½" by 6 ½")
6 cloves garlic, peeled and chopped..
½ cup fresh Italian parsley, washed,
dried and chopped
¼ Cup Grated Pecorino Romano Cheese
¼ cup Bread Crumbs, plain
Olive Oil, Raisins, Sea Salt & Black Pepper

1. Once the beef has been cut, lay all the pieces out on a clean table. Lightly season the beef with salt & pepper.

2. Drizzle a little olive oil over each piece of beef. Evenly distribute chopped Parsley over all the Beef.

3. Evenly distribute the Pecorino Cheese over all the beef.

4. Sprinkle Bread Crumbs over Beef. Put to raisons on to each slice of Beef.

5. Roll each piece of beef Jelly-Roll style. Take two toothpicks for each piece of beef and fasten each piece of beef closed with the toothpicks.

6. Lightly salt & pepper the outside of each rolled piece of beef.

7. Brown all the Beef Rolls (Braciole) in a pan with

Olive Oil. Once all the beef is nicely browned, put all the Beef Braciole into tomato sauce or meat gravy that you have already started.

NOTE: If making just Beef Braciole on their own and not with any other meat, you will have started a basic tomato sauce using 4-5 28 ounce cans of tomato, and once the sauce has begun to cook you will brown the Braciole in a pan, then add the Braciole to pot with tomatoes and simmer over low heat for 2 ½ hours until the Braciole are tender.

Also take note. Not many people do this, but you can cook the Braciole without sauce, by simple slow roasting them in the oven at 325 degrees for an hour and a half or so, until the Braciole are tender.

You can then serve the Braciole with their cooking juices of olive oil and a little bit of water and meat juices. Yumm! Serve the Braciole with some roast potatoes and a salad if you like. And these roast Braciole or Braciole cooked in "Sauce" are great sliced and served as a Sandwich with the, their cooking juices.

This recipe can also be made with Pork Braciole, which if I'm making Braciola on it's own I prefer Pork Braciole, but if I'm making a Sunday Sauce with with Sausage and Pork Ribs, I prefer to make Beef Braciole for the Sunday Sauce "Gravy."

Note: If you're wondering why sometimes it's written Braciola & sometimes Braciole? Braciola is singular, while Braciole is the plural form of Braciola. Basta.

"Italy? Anywhere and everywhere you go? It's great! "The Most Beautiful of Beauty, The World's Tastiest Food, and most Marvelous Wine, Art, Style, and Grace. It's Italy! You can't go Wrong!"

DBZ

SUNDAY SAUCE alla CLEMENZA

"Hey come over here kid. Learn something. You never know when you're gonna have to cook for 20 guys some day. You see, you start out with a little oil. Then you fry some garlic. Then you throw in some tomatoes, tomato paste, you fry it, you make sure it doesn't stick. You get it to a boil. You Shove in your Sausage and Meatballs, Hey? Add a bit of Wine, a little sugar, you see? And that's my trick."

Peter Clemenza,
The Godfather

This is a famous scene in The Godfather, one of the greatest movies ever and especially loved by Italian Americans. It's by Italian-American Director Francis Ford Coppola and writer Mario Puzo, and starring Al Pacino as Michael Corleone, co-starring Richard Castellano as Clemenza who makes his famed Sunday Sauce Gravy alla Clemenza.

Meatballs alla Clemenza

INGREDIENTS:

1 lb. ground Beef
½ lb. ground Veal, ½ lb. Ground Pork
4 Tbs. fresh Italian Parsley, chopped
1 minced onion, 2 cloves garlic, minced
4 Tablespoons plain breadcrumbs
2 large eggs, ¼ cup Milk
Salt & Pepper, ½ cup grated Parmigiano or Pecorino

PREPARATION:

1. In a small bowl, break and beat eggs. Add bread-crumbs and milk and let soak for 10 minutes.

2. In a large bowl, add all the remaining ingredients. Add eggs and mix well with your hands.

3. Shape meat mixture to from balls that are about 3 inches in diameter.

4. Coat the bottom of a cookie sheet or roasting pan with a thin film of olive oil. Cook Meatballs at 350 degrees for 10 minutes.

5. Take meatballs out of oven and simmer on low heat for 45 minutes in a batch of Tomato Sauce or Sunday Sauce (Gravy).

THE SAUCE

INGREDIENTS:

10 to 12 Sweet Italian Pork Sausages
(or ½ Sweet and half Hot Sausages)
1 medium Onion, peeled and chopped fine
8 Cloves garlic, peeled and finely chopped
¼ Cup Olive Oil
5-28 ounce Cans Whole San Marzano Tomatoes or other good quality tomatoes. Puree or finely chop 3 of the cans of tomatoes and leave 2 cans tomatoes chunky 1/2 small can Tomato Paste, 1 teaspoon Pepperoncino
1 tablespoon Black Pepper, and 1 Teaspoon Salt
1 teaspoon Sugar
And a Bit O' Wine (1/4 cup Red Wine)
1 Batch of *Meatballs* from the recipe on page 68

1. Brown the Sausages in a large pot with three tablespoons olive oil, over medium heat for about 8-10 minutes. Remove to a plate and set aside.

2. Add remaining olive oil to pot. Lower heat to low. Add the garlic and cook for about 3 minutes.

3. *"Add Tomato Paste Fry with Garlic. You make sure it doesn't stick"* (just like Clemenza*). "Add your tomatoes, continue frying, Then you Shove-In your Sausage & Meatballs, add o' bit of Wine, a little Sugar, and that's Clemenza's Trick."*

4. Simmer for 1 ½ hour at lowest heat level possible and it's done, *Sunday Sauce alla Clemenza.*

GRAVY !!!
alla Momma DiMaggio

They say this dish was Joe DiMaggio's favorite. Joltin Joe DiMaggio, The Yankee Clipper, and greatest Italian-American to ever sport a Major League Baseball Uniform. Yes, "Joe D" was Italian-American, and being so, you know Joe loved his maccheroni, Meatballs, Sausage, Spaghetti Vongole, Mussels, and Baked Clams.

The recipe is from Joe D's mom's, Rosaria Mecurio DiMaggio who fed Joe this dish as a boy, a young man, and as a New York Yankee. They say, Momma DiMaggio tried unsuccessfully to teach Joe's wife *Marilyn Monroe* how to make the *"Sauce"* that Joe liked so much, but Marilyn could not get a handle on the dish, she being without the Italian touch. Oh, well, maybe that's why the split up? Italians are very picky about their food. "Just kidding!" Anyway, maybe you could do what Marilyn Monroe couldn't, learn how to make the DiMaggio Family Sunday Sauce Gravy, the kind so well loved by Joltin Joe himself, Joe DiMaggio, and his mother's tasty recipe right here.

GRAVY alla ROSARIA DiMAGGIO

Ingredients:

1 - 1 ½ to 2 pound piece of Veal Shank
2 medium Onions, chopped fine
Olive Oil
8 cloves Garlic, finely chopped
¼ teaspoon Pepperoncino (Red Pepper Flakes)
Salt & Pepper to taste
5 – 28 ounce cans crushed Tomatoes
1 28 ounce can Tomato Puree
4 tablespoons Tomato Paste
1 cup water
10 links Italian Sweet Sausage
1 batch of Meatballs from previous Meatball recipe

1. Season Veal Shank with salt & black pepper.
Place ¼ cup olive oil in a large pot and brown the
Veal Shank over high heat until the shank is nicely
browned on both sides (12 minutes).

2. Lower heat and add the onions. Cook onions on
low heat for 4 minutes. Add garlic and cook over
low heat for 3 minutes.

3. Turn heat up to high and add 1 can of chopped
tomatoes. Cook over high heat for 5 minutes. Add
remaining tomato products and water. Bring the
sauce up to the boil. When the sauce comes to a boil,
lower the heat to very low. Season with salt & black
pepper.

4. Simmer *Sauce* with the Veal Shank for 1 hour and 45 minutes, stirring sauce occasionally so the sauce won't stick to bottom of pot and burn.

5. When the sauce has been simmering for 55 minutes, you can start to lightly brown the sausages in a separate pan. Brown nicely, drain off oil and add the browned Sausages to the pot of sauce. Cook 30 minutes.

5. After you put the sausages into the pot, make the meatball recipe from previous pages. Mix the ground meats with seasonings to make the meatballs. Shape the meatballs, then brown in the pan you cooked the sausages in.

6. Add the browned Meatballs to the "Sauce" after the sauce has been simmering for at least 2 hours and a half to an hour and 15 minutes. After browning the Meatballs, add to pot with Sauce and continue cooking the "Sauce" over low heat for another 35 minutes until the meatballs and sausages are cooked through and the Veal Shank has become nice and tender. Total cooking time is 2 ¾ to 3 ½ hours.

NOTE: This "Sauce" (aka Gravy) is best with a short pasta like Rigatoni. You can serve this dish by first serving pasta without the meats, but dressed with the sauce. Then serve the Meats second as the Main-Course without the Pasta, but with boiled potatoes, polenta, or sautéed green vegetables. Your second option, which most people do is to serve the dish in one course with Pasta, Sauce, and Meats. Whatever way you like, it's tasty as heck all the same. Buon Appetito

GOODFELLAS

Big Paulie: *"Don't put too many onions in the Sauce Vinny!"*

Vinny: *"I didn't Paul. I put 3 small onions, that's all!"*

Johnny Dio: *"3 Onions? How many cans of tomatoes did you use?"*

Vinny: *"Two."*

Johnny Dio: *"That's too many onions!"*

After the scene in The *Godfather* with *Clemenza* showing *Michael* how to make *"Sauce,"* and the construction of the *Timballo in Big Night*, the prison dinner scene in Goodfellas is one of the most famous of all. Johhnny Dio is cooking up Steaks, as Big Paulie slices garlic razor thin and lectures Vinny on how many onions go in the "Sauce."

Myself, I like to use a good amount of onions just like Vinny, who is played by Goodfellas director *Martin Scorsese's* father *Charlie*. When it comes to *"Gravy"* a.k.a. Sunday Sauce, or simply *"Sauce,"* there are almost as many different recipes and versions as there are cooks who make them.

You can make yours according to your own taste and family traditions, and put more or less onions and garlic, with Pork Ribs like mine, or not, with Sausages, Meatballs, and Braciole (the most popular), or just with Sausage & Meatballs like Clemenza's Godfather Mob War Sauce. Just make it good. Use one of the recipes in this book, as a starting point and alter it to your own taste if you like.

"If your Mother Cooks Italian Food, why should you go to a restaurant?"

Martin Scorsese on Mom Dolly

"So true Marty, and that is exactly what this book is all about."

Goodfellas Sauce *alla Prigione*

1 Veal Shank, 1 1/2 lbs. Pork Country Ribs
1 ½ pounds Sweet Italian Sausage
Meatballs (Meatball recipe page 44)
6 – 28 oz. cans Crushed Tomatoes & 28 oz. water
8 cloves of Garlic sliced paper-thin *Big-Paulie Style*
3 small Onions, chopped fine
1 cup Dry Red Wine (prefer Chianti)

1. Season Veal Shank & Ribs with Salt & Pepper and brown in a large frying pan in ¼ cup of Olive Oil on all sides until nice and gold and brown, about 12 minutes.

2. Remove meats from pot and set aside. Add onions and cook for 4 minutes on low heat. Add garlic cook 2 minutes.

3. Put Ribs and Veal Shank back in the pot, add wine and cook over high heat until reduced by half (10 Minutes).

4. Add tomatoes and 2 cups of water, bring to the boil, and then lower to a low simmer. Simmer 1 ½ hours.

5. Brown sausages over medium heat until nice and brown. Add to sauce and cook for 25 minutes.

6. Brown the Meatballs, then add to Sauce and cook for 35 minutes on low heat. Sauce is done. Total cooking time about 2 hours and 45 minutes. Serve with Rigatoni or whatever maccheroni that you like.

"Spaghetti is Love."

.... Mario Batali

SUNDAY SAUCE alla BELLINO

This is my Sunday Sauce recipe. I love adding pork spareribs, which not too many people do. I heard about putting spareribs into the Gravy one day, it sounded great, as I do love Pork Ribs. Who doesn't? Made it with the ribs one day and the *Sauce* came out great and the Ribs were absolutely phenomenal. When the ribs cook in the sauce and become nice and tender, the taste is amazing. Anyone who has ever tasted my Sauce, really goes nuts for the pork ribs, which most have never had, and are amazed by the wonderful flavor. And of course, there's the Sausage & Meatballs. "Yumm!" We love Braciole, when making my *Sauce,* I always make it with; Sausages, Meatballs, and the Ribs, but not always with the Braciole. So depending what you like, you can do the same, making the Gravy with these four meat components; the Sausages, Meatballs, Braciole, and the Pork Ribs. You can make the Sunday Sauce with just Meatballs and Sausages, whereby you would cut down the amount of tomatoes by a couple cans. Make it anyway you want, keeping in mind, you must have at least two of the meat components or it's not a Sunday Sauce.

As well as the following Sunday Sauce Gravy recipe of mine, you can add Pork Neck, which many people do, as do I sometimes. You can also throw in a Veal Shank like Joe D's Mom, and even chicken thighs (I do this sometimes as well) if you like. It's all good, and oh-so-tasty, it's Sunday Sauce, aka *Gravy*!

The Recipe: Sunday Sauce alla Bellino

Ingredients:

½ cup olive oil
2 medium onions, minced
12 cloves garlic, minced
7-28 oz. cans of crushed tomatoes
1 ½ pounds Pork Neck
2 lbs. Pork Spareribs
2 lbs. Sweet Italian sausage
2 cups chicken broth
1 Teaspoon crushed red pepper
1 ½ teaspoons salt
1 tablespoon black pepper
1 batch of Meatballs from this book's Meatball recipe

1. Place onions in olive oil in a large pot (at least 12 quarts). Sauté on a low flame for 5 minutes. Add garlic and cook for 3 minutes on low heat.

2. Add all the tomatoes. Raise flame to high. Bring the tomatoes up to the boil, then lower the sauce to a very low simmer. Fill 1 can with water and add to sauce. Don't worry, the water will evaporate. Adding the water helps enable the sauce to cook without burning.

3. Season Pork Neck with salt & pepper. Brown Pork Neck in a separate pan over medium heat until nicely browned, about 10 minutes. Add to pot with tomatoes.

4. Cut in-between rib bones so you have pairs of 2 ribs each. Brown the ribs in the pan you browned the pork neck in. After browning put ribs in pot with the Sauce.

5. Simmer the Sauce over a low flame for 1 3/4 hours, stirring occasionally.

6. Place the Sausages in the pan that you browned the ribs in. Brown the sausages in pan over medium heat. Make sure to get a nice medium browning on the sausages, but be careful not to over cook. Once sausages are all nicely brown but still raw inside, remove from pan and add to pot with the sauce. Let cook 30 minutes in sauce.

7. While the sauce is simmering, make meatballs from the Meatball recipe (page 44). When the sauce has been cooking for 2-1/4 hours, place the meatballs in a 350 degree oven for 12 minutes to brown slightly.

8. Add the browned meatballs to the *Gravy*.

9. Let the sauce continue cooking for 30 minutes until the meatballs are cooked through. When stirring, be careful not to break the meatballs.

10. Serve the sauce with your favorite Short Pasta such as Rigatoni, Gnocchi, or Ziti. Or serve pasta as a first course with just the sauce and no meat. Then serve meats and Gravy as the main course with boiled potatoes or polenta.

NOTE: The sauce should simmer on a very low flame. It is important to stir the bottom of the pot with a wooden spoon every few minutes to keep the sauce from burning. If sauce gets too thick you can add a little water which will evaporate as it cooks.

WHAT WINE for SUNDAY SAUCE

Wine for Sunday Sauce? What do you drink? Which wine pairs best with Sunday Sauce, the Supreme Dish of Italian-America? Is it Chianti, most iconic of all Italian Wines? Perhaps Aglianico or Piedirosso from the region of Campania where the roots of Italian-American Sunday Sauce Gravy begin? Or a Sicilian Wine like Nero d'Avola, Frapatto, Nerello Mascales? If you trace the roots of Italian-American Sunday Sauce and the people who created it, Sicilians are among the top of the list, so it could be a Sicilian Etna Rosso, Frapatto, or Cersaulo di Vittoria. Or, how bout a jug of Carlo Rossi Paisano? Carlo Rossi Pasiano, what? "Are you kidding," you say? No, not really. Yes I know, Carlo Rossi "Paisano" just had to catch your eye. And I'm sure most of you are asking the question, "Carlo Rossi Paisano, are you joking?" The answer. "No!" Well I'm not saying it's the best choice. No, I'm not joking, just trying to make a point and I'll tell you why.

I'm here to tell you, it can be one or more of many wines, "a nice Chianti," as Anthony Hopkins might say, Aglianico from Campania and Napoli, maybe a Barbera from Piedmont, and yes even Carlo Rossi a jug wine from California and considered the lowliest of wines, but not really. Listen, Carlo Rossi could be your wine, maybe not. Now, let me tell you something, I myself have drank some of the World's Priciest, and so-called *greatest wines in the World,*

Trophy Wines, like; Sassicaia, Gaja Barbaresco. La Tache, Chateau Petrus, Chateau Haute Brion, Petrus, Chateau Cheval Blanc, Chateau Latour, all the great Brunello and Barolo wines, great vintage Champagnes, you name it, "I've had it." And with my knowledge of wine, I can tell you, a lot of it is hype, and Marketing BS, and sometimes not. And I'll tell you this, do not be so much of a snob, a Wine Snob. You see that Carlo Rossi, with all the prestigious wines that I've consumed over the years, I'm not above drinking that, Carlo Rossi. The wine has special meaning and affection for me. It's one of the two wines my uncles always bought for our Sunday Family Meals. Meals of Meatballs, Sunday Sauce "Gravy," Ravioli, Veal Marsala, Chicken Cacciatore, whatever. My Uncles Tony and Frank always had either Carlo Rossi Paisano or Gallo Hearty Burgundy on hand. They were their go-to wines, and they only had other wines if someone brought something like a bottle of Bolla Valpolicella, Ruffino Chianti or some other wine. Now don't get me wrong, I'm not saying Paisano or Gallo Hearty Burgundy are great wines, "No." But they are not that bad, they are Italian-American, as is Sunday Sauce, these wines are made by Italian-Americans and they have social significance to we Americans of Italian ancestry. These wines are part of our history, as are the wines from the great Robert Mondavi, Macari Vineyards, The Mondavi Family, Francis Ford Coppola and other Italian Families who make wine in America.

So what the Hell am I saying you ask? What wines to drink with the Sunday Sauce or any homemade Italian American Meal? Well, actually most of the time I do drink wines from Italy with my Sunday Sauce or whatever Italian food we're making. The Carlo Rossi is just when we eat over Uncle Tony's house with Uncle Frank and all the wonderful meals with Aunt Fran, Aunt Helen, Mommy, Cousin Tony, and my brothers and sister and the whole family. No, I'm not above drinking Carlo Rossi or Gallo if my Uncles are serving it, if it's good enough for them, it's good enough for me. Heck, those guys who all fought in World War II, my mother's brothers; James, Tony, and Frank Bellino did. They were of "The Greatest Generation," so they say. Of all the great meals I've had over the years; in Rome, in Verona, Greve, Hong Kong, Paris, Saigon, New York. I've enjoyed them all, but none more than the ones on Grove Street in Lodi, New Jersey at my Aunt Fran and Uncle Tony's house, or at Aunt Helen's, or Uncle Jimmy and Aunt Wanda's. We ate many a Sunday Sauce laden with Sausage, Meatballs, Braciole, and the wine? Yes, Gallo Hearty Burgundy or a jug of Carlo Rossi. They were good for me then, and if I'm eating with my uncles, "God Bless Them," they're in their 90s (years old), yes, I will drink from the "Jug."

When I'm not in Jersey and eating with my Aunts, Uncles, Cousins, and I'm at home in Greenwich Village I'm usually drinking Chianti, most times, sometimes Barolo, Barbera, Brunello, or perhaps a bottle of Macari "Collina," a nice Italian-Style Wine made by an Italian-American family on the North Fork of Long Island. The Collina is perfect for Sunday Sauce. Yes, I like drinking Collina, or Aglainico, an Etna Rosso from Sicily, but the wine I love and like to drink most often is Chianti. I fell in love with Chianti on my first trip to the region back in 1988. The Chianti Classico wine region is absolutely gorgeous with vineyards of rows of mythical Sangiovese Vines, rolling hills, castles, stone farm houses hundreds of years old, Cypress Trees dotting the peaks of hills, the Chiantigiana Roma Road and one gorgeous scene after the other. Oh, yes, by the way, Chianti is the name of the region and the wine is named after the region.

Chianti goes well with just about anything we eat, especially Meatballs, Sausage, and Sunday Sauce. Chianti comes from Tuscany and is a medium bodied wine made mostly from Sangiovese (The Blood of Jobe), and with small percentages of other native Tuscan grapes like; Colorino, Malvasia Nero, Canaiolo, or Ciliegiolo. The wine is a marvel that will literally pair well with just about any dish of the vast Italian repertoire. So no matter what you make, if it's Wedding Soup, Fettuccine Bolognese, Sunday Sauce, or Sausage & Peppers, it's a safe bet that Chianti will go well with it.

One thing I must say, and I would like to impress upon people I talk to, is that I usually don't like wines like big, concentrated Cabernet Sauvignon or Syrah from California or Australia. To me, these are the last wines I would ever want to drink with Italian food, and I recommend you do too, if you're looking for the best experience possible. The reason? These wines are usually very rich, thick and heavy, and because of that, they clash with the food instead of complementing them. The wines you want to drink should have good flavor, but should be light to medium in body and weight, not Big, Fat, Rich, and concentrated. That's "No Bueno!" So for Sunday Sauce and most Italian Food, go for wines like; Chianti, a light Barbera, or Ruche, and yes even Carlo Rossi, but not rose.

"You see, I was cooking dinner that night. I had to start braising Beef, Pork Butt, and Veal Shanks for the Tomato Sauce. It was Michael's favorite. I was making Ziti with Meat Gravy and I'm planning to roast peppers over the flames and I was gonna put on some string beans with some olive oil and garlic and I have some beautiful cutlets that were cut just right that I was gonna fry up before dinner just as an appetizer" ...

*Ray Liotta as Henry Hill
in Martin Scorsese's Goodfellas*

MEATBALL PARM MONDAYS

The Meatball Parm Sandwich, as stated earlier, is one of thee Italian-American males most *treasured* of all things in his life. Things he needs to live a happy, normal, satisfying life, and an actual necessity for true *Happiness.* It's right up there with Mom, Grandma, your Girl, wine, Sausages, and Sunday Sauce. "We ask not for much."

No you do not have to be a Man or a Boy to eat one. Ladies and Girls eat them as well. It's just that the male of the species happens to eat 5-times the amount that Italian-American females do. Not only that, but the male of the species holds Meatballs and Meatball Parms in much Greater Reverence, than do Italian females. They "Exalt" it, as the Meatball Parm, it deserves such adulation. The men and boys adore it and get quite excited at the prospect and act of eating one, the "Meatball Parm." And the ladies who make them, know how much their boys love and cherish meatballs and the Meatball Parm Sandwich. Italian women want to please their men, their sons, so they make them tasty bowls of pasta, Sunday Sauce, Sausage & Peppers and Meatball Parm Sandwich when their men desire them. Yes, we don't need much; friends, family, good food and wine, and we're happy.

Yes it's true, Italian-American ladies and girls like this thing called the Meatball Parm as well, but they don't get quite as excited about this sandwich as do the men & boys do. You see, Meatball Parms are held quite dear to Italian men. Yes, it's a guy thing, and more specifically, an "Italian Guy Thing." Yes, Italian-American males have given the Meatball Parm Iconic Status within our lives and the realm of food. Why? We're Italian, it's as simple as that.

The Great Ritual of the Meatball Parm Monday and as it ties to the Sunday Sauce. You make the Meatballs for the Sauce, the *Gravy*. On Saturday you will buy all the meat; the Sausages and the rest of the ingredients for your Sunday Sauce (Gravy) to be made on Sunday. However, on Saturday you are already thinking about those Meatball Parms for Monday's lunch.

Yes, we do Meatball Parms on Monday, following the previous days Sunday Sauce. You see, you have to think ahead. Every good Italian knows that when you go through all the effort and time it will take to make a pot of Sunday Sauce Gravy. You don't just make it for Sunday's consumption alone. No, that would be a waste of time to make just enough to eat on Sunday. Well, it wouldn't be a waste of time, but your time will be better spent if you make more. It takes time, effort, energy, and work to make a Sunday Sauce, which of course is well worth the effort. You do not mind the work involved at all, for in the end, the *"Rewards are Great."* A Sunday Sauce will yield, the beloved Sausages, Gravy, Braciole, succulent Ribs, and Meatballs for Monday's Meatball Parms.

It does not really take much more time to make a larger quantity in order to have leftovers for the next day or two, and this is just what one wants to do, which is to keep the *Sauce* going, and going for another day, even two. And in those leftovers are the much *Prized* Meatballs for Monday's Lunch of Meatball Parm Sandwiches. Yes, the men love and need Meatball Parms on Monday, for the ritual of the Meatball Parms on Monday is a *Time-Honored* tradition enjoyed by many. As the saying goes, "The Simple Pleasure of Life," here it is quite apropos.

So, you see, on Saturday when one goes to buy the ingredients to make the Gravy, they automatically know to make sure they get enough ground meat to make plenty of Meatballs that will last the Sunday Supper as well as yielding numerous leftover Meatballs for Monday's Meatball Parms. And there's always assaults on the pot of dipping in and grabbing meatballs before you even sit down to the table. With Meatballs and Gravy, temptations are always great. Yes the men, methodically make sure that there are enough leftover meatballs for Monday's lunch. When all are finished eating the great *Sauce* on Sunday, they set some Meatballs aside for the next days ritual of Meatball Sandwiches for lunch. These sandwiches will make any dreaded Monday *so much better*, that's for sure.

And if there are leftover Sausages? On Tuesday one can make Spaghetti or Rigatoni with Sauce and Sausages, or even a Sausage Sandwich. Think ahead boys and girls, think of Monday and your Meatball Parm.

The "MEATBALL PARM"
.... and How to Make One

Ingredients:

4 Hero Rolls or 1 large Loaf of Italian Bread, cut in half lengthwise
12 Meatballs and Sauce they cooked in
1 pound sliced Mozzarella Cheese or sliced Provolone
1/3 cup grated Parmigiano Reggiano

1. Put the meatballs and sauce in a pot. Cook the Meatballs in the Sauce on a low flame for 15 to twenty minutes, until the meatballs are heated through.

2. Place bottom parts of bread in 375 degree oven for 6 minutes to heat and brown lightly, being careful not to let the bread burn. Seven minutes before the meatballs will be finished heating, place the sliced Mozzarella or Provolone on the top part of hero rolls or bread. Place in oven to let the cheese melt and slightly brown, about 7-8 minutes.

3. When the Meatballs and sauce are done cooking remove from stove.

4. Assemble Meatball Parm Sandwiches by laying out the 4 bottom pieces of Bread (Rolls) on a work surface.

5. Spoon a moderate coating of Tomato Sauce over the top part of the bottom pieces of bread, and sprinkle a little grated cheese over the tomato sauce. Place 3 Meatballs on top of each Hero Roll or all 12 over the whole of your large loaf of Italian Bread. Cover the Meatballs with some more sauce, then sprinkle remaining grated Parmigiano on top. Place tops of Bread with the melted cheese over the meatballs and press down lightly. Serve and Enjoy this great experience.

ITALIAN SANDWICHES

Sandwiches? Italian Sandwiches, are held dear in the Italian-American enclave. Yes we've already touched on one great Italian-Sandwich, Italian-American Sandwich that is, for there is quite a difference between a sandwich made in Italy and one made by Italian-Americans in America. The biggest difference is in the size. You probably know that an Italian-American Sandwich, especially the Subs are gonna be a lot bigger than their Italian brethren back in Italy. Yes, you would be right. Another difference between sandwiches (Panini) made in the Mother Country Italy and those made by Italian-Americans, is the difference in the way we incorporate them into the daily diet. In Italy, the sandwiches (Panini) are much smaller. We've already established that. The way they are most often eaten in Italy are as a "snack" in-between meals, thus a good reason for them to be smaller. There is one particular sandwich they make in Italy that I fell in love with at the first meal I ever had in my beloved ancestral country Italia, way back in 1985. That type of sandwich is known as the Tramezzini, a sandwich you "never" see in America. These Tramezzini Sandwiches are most often found in Bars and Caffes in Italy, and are prepared ahead of time and on display in a counter at the bar. There is always an array of all sorts of assorted Tramezzini with different fillings in each, and they are all quite tempting as they are laid out before your eyes. It is hard to resist getting two or three of these scrumptious little morsels when at a bar or Caffe.

So, the Tramezzini Sandwiches get their name from the bread they are made with, which is soft white bread, crust removed and cut in-half into triangles. One Tramezzino Sandwich amounts to what we would consider a half sandwich on white bread. There are many different fillings that are quite tasty. Some fillings are; Prosciutto and Cheese, Egg Salad with Tomato, Crab Salad, Artichoke and Hard Boiled Egg, Tuna and Tomato, and Ham, Tomato, and Mushroom just to name a few of the many possibilities.

Another popular sandwich in Italy is known simply as "Toast." Toast is also made on soft white bread. It is filled with Ham and Cheese and toasted crisp on a special panini press. It's big time snack sandwich.

Other sandwiches are made with a small round roll or small hero type roll and may be filled with Tomato and Mozzarella, Salami, Prosciutto, Mortadella and other various fillings. Also these similar ingredients might be served in-between sliced Focacacia. One thing to remember is that they don't pile on a lot of fillings as we do in America, and the sandwiches are much smaller and thinner and meant for a snack and not as a meal as in America.

Now, back to the good ol' Italian-American sandwich; The Meatball Parm, Sausage & Peppers, Chicken Parm, an Italian Sub and more. Yes, they are bigger and meant usually as a meal, and in particular for lunch or breakfast, but can be eaten any time of the day. Yes our sandwiches are much bigger. Italian American Sandwiches are on average about 4 to 5 times larger than their Italian brethren.

As we've already stated, the sandwich in the Italian-American vernacular are much more of a guy thing. One reason being, years ago, not as many women worked, they stayed at home and took care of the kids and home. The men were out working, many in Blue-Collar jobs, and when it came time to eat lunch, quite often it would be some sort of sandwich. The sandwich might often be a regular American Sandwich like Ham & Cheese, Tuna, or Turkey and Swiss, but whenever an Italian-American man gets a chance to get a sandwich from a good Italian Deli, Sandwich Shop, or Pizzeria, he might very well go for one of the Italian favorites in; a Meatball Parm, Sausage & Peppers, or Italian Sub, aka Combo, made of; Ham, Salami, and Provolone or Capicola & Provolone. If they're in New Orleans, if they don't get a Po Boy, they'll grab the famed New Orleans Sicilian Muffuletta. In Philly they'll get a Hoagie or Philly Cheesesteak, an Italian American invention, and one of America's favorites. In Chicago, they've got the famed Italian-Beef of Chicago, another Italian-American invention, invented in Chicago by Italian workers of the Union Stock Yards, who'd bring home cheap cuts of Beef that they slow cook with juices from the meat. They'd slice the Beef thin, slather with meat juices, and pile on some Italian Bread, with or without Giardiniera Salad of pickled vegetables. Way back when these Italian-Beef-Sandwiches were served at Weddings and other Italian-American gatherings;

Christenings, Birthdays, and Anniversary Celeb-
rations in Church Basements, or Italian American
Social Clubs, A great tradition and awesome
sandwich were invented, and like it's cousins; The
Philly Cheesesteak, and the Muffuletta of New
Orleans, Italian-Beef is of Chicago, and somehow
though supremely delicious, the sandwich has more
or less stayed local in Chicago and not migrated
around the country.

So you see, we Italians do love our sandwiches.
And you don't have to be Italian to eat one, all
Americans do, as America has the World's largest
Sandwich Culture of all, which no one, nowhere can
top.

SAUSAGE & PEPPERS

Sausage & Peppers are quite important in the World of Italian-America. In fact extremely important. Sausage & Peppers, can be had on a plate with some roast potatoes, which is quite nice. You can do this at home or at an Italian restaurant. Grilling Sausages at your back yard barbecue is a favorite of many, whether the Sausages are Sweet, Hot, or stuffed with parsley or Provolone or not. These are a couple of ways we Italians like our Sausages, but where Sausages and Sausages & Peppers to be more specific really shine, and receive legendary status is as a sandwich of Sausage & Peppers at your favorite Italian-Deli, Pizzeria, Pork Store, or any one of the many Italian Feast held around New York, Boston, Philly, Jersey, Chicago, Baltimore and more. When it comes to sausages, though we may love our Orecchiette with Broccoli Rabe & Sausage, it is our beloved Sausage & Peppers, "The Sandwich" that we love best. And as with the Meatball Parm Sandwich, it is the male of the species that loves them most, and by a very long shot at that. Listen I don't mean to beat this point to the bush as they say, but it's fact, Italian guys love there Sunday Sauce and there sandwiches, and much more so than the ladies. It's just pure and simple fact.

Men working hard all day, when the mid-day hour comes along, these men might very well find themselves at their favorite Italian Deli or Pork Store getting a nice hefty helping of some tasty Sausage and Peppers, the sandwich Yes we love these babies so. What's not to love? Some properly made sweet or hot Italian Sausages cooked on a flat-top grill with slowly sautéed peppers and onion stuffed between a good piece of warmed Italian Bread, and you're set. What can be better? Not too much more, and as good as they are, if you'd ask for more than that, it's a form of a Sin of greed. Yes it would. You see, a good Sausage & Pepper Sandwich is that good, as the Big Boys will tell you, "Fougettabout-itt!!!"

The sausages and where they come from, is an all important task in procuring *the best*. They've gotta be. If you're making some Sausage & Pepper Sandwiches at home, or you're getting one at the deli or Pizzeria, or one of the best places to get them of all, "The Italian Feast" such as The Feast of San Genaro in New York's Little Italy held every year in the first week and a half of September. I love *Lucy's,* a stand that makes one of the best Sausages & Pepper Sandwiches you'd ever taste, anywhere.

And like the Meatball Parm, the Sausage & Pepper Sandwich is held in mythically high-esteem. Whether you are making your own at home, having one at San Gennaro's on Mulberry Street, at the St. Anthony's Feast in Greenwich Village, or Our Lady of Pompeii on Carmine Street which is actually New York's real Little Italy (South Greenwich Village), the Sausage & Pepper Sandwich is always a treat and a *Time-Honored Italian-American Tradition* that taste so very good. So my friends, "Mangia Bene!"

SAUSAGE & PEPPERS SANDWICH

Ingredients:

8 Italian Sweet or Hot Sausages
6 tablespoons Olive Oil
2 Red Bell Peppers, 1 Green Bell Pepper
Remove inside ribs and discard, cut into ½ inch slices.
2 medium Yellow Onions, peeled and cut into ½" slices
Salt & Black Pepper
4 Hero Rolls or 1 Large Loaf Italian Bread large enough to make 4 Sandwiches
2 large Frying Pans that don't have plastic or rubber handles. 1 to Cook Sausages and 1 to cook Peppers & Onions

1. Place 1 tablespoon of olive in one frying pan. Put Sausages in this pan and turn heat on to low-medium flame. Prick each sausage link with the tip of a knife so skins won't burst when cooking. Cook Sausages for about 12 minutes on top of stove, turning so they brown on all four sides. Place Sausages in a 350 degree oven and continue cooking for about 12 minutes.

2. Place remaining olive oil in second pan. Add Peppers and cook over medium flame, cook for 10 minutes while stirring occasionally. Add onions and cook Peppers and Onions, season with Salt & Black

Pepper, mix. Cook over medium Flame for 5 minutes while stirring occasionally. Place and cook in 350 degree oven for 10 minutes.

3. When the Sausages, Peppers and onions are finished cooking, remove from oven, and let cool slightly for 3 minutes while you split the Italian Bread or Hero Rolls in half lengthwise.

4. Place a small amount of Peppers and Onions over bottom part of each hero roll. Place 2 Sausages on top of the bottom part of Hero Rolls or Bread that is topped with Peppers & Onions. With the remaining Peppers and Onions, divide into 4 equal parts and cover all the sausages. Top with top of Hero Roll or Bread, and Enjoy your Sausage & Pepper Sandwich, "Italian-American Style" !!!

SAUSAGE POTATO & EGG

The Sausage Potato & Egg Sandwich is not nearly as popular as the previous two sandwiches which are Italian-American *favorites* as well as being favorites of all Americans, be they Italian or not. This Sausage Potato & Egg Sandwich is real tasty, and a sandwich that's not as well known in the larger American public, but mostly amongst Italian-Americans. Hey, we have to keep some things to ourselves. Yes, the sandwich is real tasty and is best known as a lunch-time sandwich served at Italian Delis mainly in the north-east. Though most well-known for lunch, this sandwich is great any time of the day. It makes a wonderful breakfast sandwich, which you would make smaller than for lunch, probably on a Kaiser Roll. You can have one for dinner, which you might precede with a hot bowl of Minestrone or Pasta Fazool. In the Italian-American community, the Sausage Potato & Egg or Sausage Pepper & Egg is quite famous as a late night snack, it really does the trick.

This sandwich is a main-stay of Italian Americans on Long Island, where there are few incredible Pork Stores and Italian Delis opened by Italians who migrated from; Brooklyn, The Bronx, and lower Manhattan, bought homes out on the Island and opened up some great Italian Food Emporiums on the Island. So, you see, they eat Italian well out there too.

SAUSAGE POTATO & EGG

Ingredients:

4 Italian Sweet Sausage links
1 large Idaho or Maine Potato, peeled and cut into
1/8" half-moon slices
1 medium Onion, peeled and cut to medium dice
4 tablespoons Olive Oil, Salt & Black Pepper
3 Jumbo Eggs, seasoned with Salt & Pepper
and beaten
2 Italian Hero Rolls or Italian Bread or 4 Hard Rolls

1. Cook Sausages in a small heavy bottom frying pan over a low flame for 12 – 15 minutes, until cooked through. Set aside to cool slightly, then cut into ¼ inch slices on the diagonal.

2. While Sausages are cooking, cook potatoes in a pot of boiling salted water for about 5 minutes until potatoes are tender but slightly firm. Remove from heat and drain potatoes dry.

3. Place 4 tbs. Olive Oil in a large non-stick frying pan. Add diced Onions and cook over low heat for 4 minutes. Add Sausages and boiled potatoes, season with salt & Pepper and cook for two minutes. Turn heat up to high, let cook for one minute, Add Eggs and cook over high-heat while stirring constantly with a wooden spoon. Cook until eggs have lost all rawness.

4. Divide evenly amongst the 2 Hero Rolls or 4 Hard Rolls, whatever you are using, or 1 large loaf of Italian Bread.

Note: If you'd like you can add a cooked Green or Red Bell Pepper to this sandwich to make a Sausage Pepper Potato & Egg Sandwich. Or you can add Pepper and omit the potato for a Sausage Pepper & Egg Sandwich.

"Most everybody who is Italian is half Italian. Except me, I'm all Italian. Mostly Sicilian, and I have a little bit of Neapolitan in me. You get you full dose with me."

The AUNT HELEN SPECIAL
"a SANDWICH"

Created by my Aunt Helen Cavalo, the secret success of this tasty sandwich is in the simplicity and having greatest quality ingredients possible, like; fresh butter, a great roll, *making it with love,* like Aunt Helen, and the best Parmigiano money can buy. Enjoy!

INGREDIENTS:

2 small Italian Hero Rolls or Any Roll You Like
4 large Eggs
Salt & Black Pepper
1 ½ cups chopped cooked Spinach (fresh or frozen)
½ cup grated Parmigiano Reggiano or Grana Padano
2 tablespoons Olive Oil, 1 tablespoon Butter

1. Beat eggs with Salt & Pepper to taste.

2. Sauté spinach for 3-4 minute low heat. Season with Salt & Pepper.

3. Place eggs in a bowl. Add grated cheese, Salt & Pepper, and beat eggs with a fork.

4. Turn heat up to high. Add eggs and cook over high heat while constantly stirring eggs with a wooden spoon or rubber spatula until the eggs are cooked completely. Remove eggs from pan and leave on the side.

5. Add a tiny bit each of olive oil and butter to pan and toast the rolls in the pan until all four halves rolls are lightly toasted.

6. Place the 2 bottoms of the rolls on plates, divide the scrambled eggs and spinach in to 2 equal parts and place on each bottom half of toasted rolls. If you like at this point you can sprinkle a bit of Salt & pepper over the eggs then top with a bit more Parmigiano. Top with top of roll, cut each sandwich in half, and enjoy. You your friends will love this one.

Note: As stated before, you can serve these eggs on toasted Crostini Bread at a cocktail hour or as the Antipasto or part of Antipasto Misto for the first course of a meal. You can also serve the Uovo Strapazetti (Scrambled Eggs) on a plate by themselves, with a Salad or some other vegetable on the side. Whatever you do, you will be surprised how much flavor and how tasty this simple, versatile dish is. Buon Appetito!

FRIED EGG & PROSCIUTTO

Fried Egg & Prosciutto? It's actually a sandwich I invented one day when I had my restaurant Bar Cichetti in New York's Greenwich Village. After going in to the restaurant one morning, setting up and then getting ready for the lunch service, as usual I made a little something to eat before lunch. I made a couple fried eggs and put them on a plate with 3 pieces of Prosciutto. One of our regular customers had walked through the door and saw me walking with my plate as I went to sit at the bar to eat it. He looked at it and asked me what it was. I told him it was just a couple fried eggs and Prosciutto for my breakfast. "Looks good," he said. Well, I guess he liked the looks of it quite a bit, cause about 15 minutes later, a waitress came in the kitchen and told me that the man on table 10 wanted some fried eggs and Prosciutto. "Sure, " I said. Two minutes later the waitress came back and said the man wanted some garlic bread as well. I made him some Fettunta, Italian for garlic bread, the Italian kind, not Italian-American.

I made the garlic bread and fried eggs, put them on a plate with 3 slices of Prosciutto di Parma and sent the order out with the waitress. The guy loved it. I loved the plate myself. I created it, something simple, just putting a few wonderful Italian ingredients that I loved together. It was quick, easy, and quite tasty. The guy kept coming in and ordering this plate, I never put it on the menu or as a special (it's a great lunch or Brunch item), I just made it for this one guy and myself. Eventually the plate of fried eggs, Prosciutto and Garlic Bread morphed into a sandwich, as one day I fried an egg, toasted a roll, put the egg and some Prosciutto on and topped it with a nice slice of Pecorino Toscano. Yumm, *"it's a dam tasty sandwich, try it some time."*

The SUB

A Submarine Sandwich, also known as a "Hero" in New York, Hoagie in Philadelphia, and "Grinder" or *Combo* in New England the Mid-West & California, and a Bomber in Upstate New York. These Sandwiches consists of Italian or French Bread split down the middle in two long pieces. In between the bread goes; Salami, Cheese, Ham, sliced tomato, lettuce, and sliced onion topped with Olive Oil, Vinegar, Oregano, Salt & Pepper. This is the basic Hero Sandwich, Sub, *Hoagie* or whatever you call it depending on where you live. In Jersey they are Submarines or simply Subs. Hero Sandwiches (Northern NJ & NY) were invented around the turn of 1900's by Italian-American immigrants on the East Coast of the United States, in cities such as; New York, Boston, Portland Maine, Providence Rhode Island, Philadelphia, and Paterson, New Jersey where it is said the first Submarine Sandwich was invented by one Dominic Conti (1874-1954) an Italian immigrant from Montella, Italy a town in the province of Avellino near *Naples* (Napoli*)*, Italy where much of Italian-America's dishes come from along with Sicily, Calabria, and Abruzzo. Conti is said to have named his sandwiches Submarines after seeing a Museum Exhibition at The Paterson Museum of a recovered 1901 Submarine The Fenian Ram. As his sandwiches made on long loaves of Italian Bread resemble the Submarine, Conti named his sandwiches Submarine Sandwiches, which later became known as Subs. Conti's granddaughter says, "My grandfather came to America in 1895 from Montella, Italy. In 1910, he started an Italian Grocery Store in Paterson (Silk City), New Jersey, which was called Dominic Conti's Grocery Store on Mill Street where he was selling traditional Italian Sandwiches. His sandwiches were made from a recipe he brought with him from Italy which consisted of a long crusty roll filled with cold cuts, topped with lettuce, tomatoes, peppers, onions, Oil & Vinegar, Italian Herbs & Spices, Salt & Black Pepper. The sandwich started with a layer of cheese and ended with a layer of cheese (so the Bread wouldn't get soggy).

So these Italian Submarine Sandwiches as they are known in Jersey, are Grinders in New England, Hoagies in Philly, and in New York they're most commonly known as a Hero, of which the name is credited to New York Herald Tribune food-writer Clementine Paddle-ford in the 1930's. As far as who invented these sandwiches, there are a few different theories of who invented the first one and where it was. Some say in the sandwich was created in Scollay Square to entice Sailors stationed at the Charlestown Navy Yard in Boston, and that the term Grinder the name of the sandwich in New England (as well as the Mid-West) comes from dockworkers who were called Grinders. Another theory has the Sandwich orig-inating in Portland, Maine. We feel this last claim is is highly unlikely and that it was Dominic Conti of Montella, Italy and Paterson, New Jersey who invented this Italian-American icon. This is the theory that has been adopted by the whole country after the birth of the Submarine Sandwich in Paterson and other Italian neighborhoods of the East Coast of the country.

Now a days there are a multitude of horrible chain Sub Stands like Subway, of which the ingredient are inferior to the original sandwiches of which you can still get at any good *Italian Deli* in New York, New Jersey, in Philly, Pittsburgh, New Orleans, Boston, and Baltimore. So why would anyone ever go to Subway?

The SUBMARINE SANDWICH
"Hoagie Hero Grinder & Sub"

INGREDIENTS:

1- 10" loaf Italian Bread
8 pieces of Sopressata or Genoa Salami
4 pieces of Boiled Ham
6 pieces of Provolone Cheese
¼ thin sliced Red Onion
4-5 slices of Ripe Tomato
3-4 leaves of Boston Lettuce or shredded Iceberg
Olive Oil
Italian Red Wine Vinegar
¼ teaspoon of Oregano
Salt & Black Pepper to taste
Optional: Hot Italian Red and or Green Peppers

ASSEMBLAGE:

1. Cut bread in half lengthwise

2. Place Provolone on bottom half of bread. Place the Ham over the cheese down the length of the Sandwich. Place Salami over Ham.

3. Place lettuce over Salami down length of sandwich.
Place tomatoes over lettuce and season with Salt, Black Pepper and a bit of Oregano. Top with this with onions, then season with Olive Oil, Vinegar, Salt, Black Pepper, and Oregano.

4. Place top of bread on sandwich, cut sandwich in half, eat, and Enjoy!

NOTE: This is the most basic Sub Sandwich, made with Ham, Salami, and Cheese, usually Provolone but some have it with Swiss Cheese. We Italians usually like to add Capicola to this basic sandwich and sometimes Mortadella. Or we'll have one with Capicola, Sopressata, and Provolone. Remember to get the best quality bread you can find, the best cheese, and best meats of course. If not, your Sub just won't be as good as it can. And remember, stay away from places like Subway. For the best Sub you'll ever get, go to an Italian Deli in an Italian neighborhood and get the best Sandwich money can buy, for just about $6.00 to $7.95, Basta!

MUFFULETTA

Muffuletta the other Great Italian-American Sandwiches along with Italian Beef (Chicago), The Philly Cheese Steak (Yes it's Italian), and Subs of all kinds. Great in it's tastiness itself, however not greatly known around the United States, and it's probably best it stays that way. The Muffuletta is an Italian American Sandwich created by Italian immigrants in New Orleans, Louisiana. More specifically Sicilian Americans. It was in New Orleans French Market, an area dominated by Sicilian Farmers, workers, and Sicilian Grocery owners, and Fruit & Vegetable Purveyors in the market that the now famous Muffuletta Sandwich was first created by Sicilian immigrant Salvatore Lupo of The Central Grocery on Decatur Street in The French Market within The French Quarter of New Orleans. That's a lot of French for a Great Italian American Sandwich to be born in, wouldn't you say? But it was born at The Central Grocery on Decatur Street by Mr. Salvatore Lupo, who I'm sure could never have dreamt that so many millions of these sandwiches would be sold over the years. He was simply trying to provide his customers with a great new tasty option for their lunch, and to make a few extra bucks for his grocery store. He created one tasty masterpiece of a sandwich, that this guy has to get every time I'm in New Orleans.

So you see, all the Italian workers in and around the French Market which included farmers bringing their produce to market, then would stop for a little lunch. Most of these Sicilian farmers and truck-drivers would get Olives, Roast Peppers, Salami, and Cheese from The Central Grocery or other near by groceria. Salvatore Lupo seeing this, had the idea of combining all these different ingredients that were eaten separately from a plate, on to a sandwich all-together. Next door to Central grocery was another Groceria, Progress Grocery where the Sicilian owner named LoGiudice baked a Sicilian Bread called Muffoletta as well as other types of Sicilian Bread like long Braided Sesame and Poppy-Seeded Bread. Salvatore Lupo when thinking about making his sandwich stuffed with Sicilian Olive Salad, Salami, Ham, Mortadella and Cheese, thought that LoGiudice's Muffoletta Bread to be perfect for this sandwich. The Muffuletta was born (1906) and named after the bread it was served on, which was Muffoletta, which turned into Muffuletta or sometimes Muffaletta. This sandwich is amazing, as far as sandwiches are concerned, the Muffulletta is without question one of the World's Greatest. It ranks right up there with New York Pastrami, Philly Cheesesteaks (also Italian), Subs, Hoagie's and Hero's, all Italian Sandwiches as well.

It's funny that the Muffulletta with all its greatness never spread across America in fame. The Muffuletta is relatively unknown outside of its birthplace New Orleans and its environs. It's not, and as we've already said, it's probably best it stays that way, and stays just in New Orleans and Louisiana, along with their famed Po Boys, another great sandwich of varied ingredients. Yes, the

Muffuletta stays in New Orleans for New Orleanians and those (Me) who have traveled there and love getting one or two on each and every trip.

And if you ever want to make one at home? Well, you won't be able to get the Muffuletta Bread that the Muffuletta is made with, but you can make one just the same. Get the same bread you'd make a Sub on, send away for some Broscoli Olive Salad, go to an Italian Deli and get yourself the best quality Mortadella, Boiled Ham, Swiss Cheese (Yes Swiss Cheese), and Salami. Cut your bread in half, pile on the Meats and Cheese and top with as much of the Olive Salad as your little heart desires. Voila, the Muffuletta. Not the same as getting one at the Central Grocery, but a pretty darn good one never-the-less. And by the way, they serve Muffuletta Sandwich at many delis and restaurants all over New Orleans and Southern Louisiana, but when I go down there, I'll not get one, a Muffuletta at any place other than The Central Grocery, as they are the best, the sandwich as well as the ambiance in this beautiful 100 year old plus museum piece of Sicilian Italian American History, New Orleans and America. Bravo to Central Grocery, Bravo to Mr. Lupo.

"We were raised in an Italian household. We were very proud of being Italian. We listened to Italian Music and ate Italian Food."

Francis Ford Coppola

Gabagool !!!

Mob Guy # 1: *"Hey Paulie, I got some Gabagool !!!*

Paulie : *"Hey you STUPID JERK !"*

This is part of a scene in Francis Ford Coppola's famed Italian-American Classic, The Godfather. The scene is during Connie Corleone's Wedding to Carlo. Paulie and Mob Guy # 1 are assigned by Sonny Corleone to be guarding the outside of the Corleone Compound from any unwanted intruders (The FBI, Rival Gangs, anybody).

Mob Guy # 1 procured a couple of Gabagool Sandwiches from one of the cooks preparing the Wedding Banquet for Connie and Don Corleone's guests at Connie's Wedding. Paulie and Guy # 1 can't eat with the guest, but they are hungry, "Hey they're Italian-American!" And a couple Gabagool's will definitely fit the bill. Gabagool, a.k.a. Gabagul, or similar, is an Italian Salumi pork-product made from the neck-meat of a pig. There are several variations of the name, including; Capicola (most common), Ham Capicola, Coppa, Capocollo, and Capicollo.

"Gabagool" is slang for Capicola? It is not "slang" but Neapolitan dialect that many Italian-Americans use for Capicola, including Tony Soprano and those real-life guys who don Big Pinky

Rings.

So you wanna make a Gabagool. The preferred sandwich is on Italian Bread or a hero-roll from a great Bread Baker like, Parisi Bakers in New York's Little Italy. Then you gotta get the *Gabagool!* You get yourself top-quality Capicola from your favorite Pork Store, Satriale's if you're in North Jersey, at Di Palo's in Little Italy, or Faicco's if you're downtown New York and Greenwich Village or at their Brooklyn outpost. You're gonna want Provolone or Mozzarella. I prefer Provolone. Get some peppers, Hot Cherry Peppers like Tony Soprano, Paulie, and Silvio. Some, myself include, prefer with Roast Sweet Peppers instead. That's all you need. A Gabagool Sandwich should have 2 to 3 times as much meat (Gabagool) to cheese ratio.

To make a Gabagool Sub, you need a good sub roll or crusty Italian-Bread, and Gabagool (Capicola) of course, thin sliced Provolone, and some Salami, either, Genoa or Sopresseta. You can also add Mortadella or Prosciutto (*Proshoot*) if you like. Put the Gabagool, Provolone and any other if any Salumi product on the bottom half of your bread, top with shredded Iceberg Lettuce, add a slice of ripe Tomato, then thin sliced Red Onion, and sprinkle on Salt, Black Pepper, Oregano, Olive Oil, and Red Wine Vinegar and "you're set!" Set if you don't want it "Hot." If you do? Then again, get yourself some Hot Italian Cherry Peppers and throw them on. That's a Gabagool Sub.

If you want just a Gabagool and not a Sub, get a nice smaller roll, some roast red sweet peppers (or Hot), the Capicola, and sliced Provolone. Pile everything on between the bread, and Voila, you've got a Gabagool, just like Tony.

PS ... For a great Gabagool Sandwich in New York, go to either Faicco's Pork Store or Parisi's Italian Deli, both are downtown New York, NY.

STUFFED ARTICHOKES

Stuffed Artichokes, scary looking, some have said. No, they-are-a-thing-of-beauty! In Italian-American Cuisine, and among the Italian-American Community, the Stuffed Artichoke is a favorite and cherished dish. It's an awesome item that is much loved. Growing up in Jersey and New York, the Stuffed Artichoke was a popular item in our house, and we always loved eating it, it's special little ritual that only an Italian Stuffed Artichoke could provide, as there are certain steps to the process.

Yes, there it is, stuffed by mommy with a bread-crumbs, cheese, garlic, and herb mixture that taste oh so good. The Stuffed Artichoke, along with Eggplant Parmigiano, and Stuffed Shells were one of my mother's best dishes. As a young child watching my mother make the bread stuffing for the artichokes, stuffing them and cooking them was quite an experience. There is nothing quite like The Stuffed Artichoke in the Food World, an Italian Stuffed Artichoke that is!

My mother got her green mixing bowl, put in some Progresso Seasoned Breadcrumbs with Pecorino Romano Cheese, a bit of Olive Oil, fresh chopped Garlic, and a bit of water. She mixed everything up with her hands, then took this breadcrumb-mixture and stuffed every little crevice in that crazy looking vegetable with the seasoned breadcrumbs.

My mother Lucia, would put some chicken broth,

Olive Oil, garlic and water in the bottom of a large pot and put the artichokes in. She'd cover the pot and set it atop a very low flame on top of the stove and let the artichokes cook for about 35 minutes or so.

Yes I used to watch my mother do this, along with stuffing and tying up the Beef Braciole one by one I watched with amazement and curiosity, everything interested me.

Oh, and when those artichokes were ready. I always remember, not having my own, but always sharing a Artichoke with my mom, and pulling the leaves off, and scraping the pulp on the leaves between my top row of teeth and the bottom ones. You bit down on the leave and pulled the artichoke leaf from back to front, scraping the pulp off the leaf and into your mouth. Yes that's how you do it. For all you Italians out there, you know what I'm talking about. For many of you, this may all sound very strange, and all I can tell you is that if you've never eaten these wonderful Italian Stuffed Artichokes, "you just gotta try them." And if this all sounds strange to you, and you're saying, "What the Hell is he talking about?" Again, you've gotta try them. Then you'll know what I'm talking about. You'll understand.

How to Make Them
"STUFFED ARTICHOKES"

Ingredients:

4 large, full-size artichokes
1 lemon, halved
1 3⁄4 cups dried breadcrumbs
1 cup grated pecorino
1⁄3 cup chopped flat-leaf parsley leaves
2 tsp. kosher salt
1 tsp. freshly ground black pepper
8 cloves garlic, finely chopped
5 tbsp. extra-virgin olive oil

1. Using a serrated knife, cut off artichoke stems to create a flat bottom. Cut top thirds off artichokes, pull off tough outermost leaves, and trim tips of leaves with kitchen shears. Rub cut parts with lemon halves. Open artichoke leaves with your thumbs to make room for stuffing; set aside.

2. Heat oven to 425°. In a large bowl, combine bread- crumbs, 3⁄4 cup pecorino, parsley, salt, pepper, and garlic. Working with one artichoke at a time over bowl, sprinkle one-quarter of breadcrumb mixture over the artichoke and work it in between leaves.

3. Transfer stuffed artichoke to a shallow baking dish. Drizzle each artichoke with 1 tablespoon oil. Pour in boiling water to a depth of 1" Rub 1 tbsp. olive oil on a sheet of aluminum foil, cover artichokes with foil (oiled side down), and secure foil tightly around dish with kitchen twine.

4. Bake until a knife easily slides into the base of an artichoke, about 45 minutes. Remove foil, sprinkle tops with remaining cheese, and switch oven to broil. Broil until tops of artichokes are golden brown, about 3 minutes.

SERVES 4

Mommy's Stuffed Peppers

This was another one of my mother's finest dishes. It's a main-stay of the Italian-American table in which when eating at home you usually have it as a main course with a salad or some roast potatoes or Green Beans on the side. In an Italian-American restaurants Stuffed Peppers are most often served as a starter and used to be found often in the famed Hot Antipasto of many and Italian-American Red Sauce Restaurant of simpler times. You don't see them as much these days as you did years ago when they were quite prevalent. Never-the-less, if you're nostalgic for them, here's my mom's recipe, so go ahead and make them. You can have them once again. You can serve the stuffed peppers either way, as an appetizer (Antipasto) or main course. My mother used to make them about two times a month and we always loved them, and you will too. Here is my mom's recipe below.

LUCIA STUFFED PEPPERS

Ingredients:

1 medium onion, minced
3 cloves of garlic, minced
6 Tablespoons chopped parsley
6 Tablespoons bread crumbs
2 eggs. Salt & pepper
1 cup long grain rice
¾ lb. ground pork
¾ lb. ground beef
1 Tablespoon Dry Oregano
½ cup grated Pecorino Romano
4 Red or Green bell peppers
½ cup chicken broth
1-1/2 cups tomato sauce

Preparation for Lucia's Stuffed Peppers:

1. Cook the rice for 12 minutes in boiling water and drain.

2. Cut the tops off the peppers and reserve.

3. Mix all remaining ingredients except the Broth and sauce in a large bowl.

4. Stuff the peppers with the meat mixture and top with the Pepper tops.

5. Place the peppers in a small baking pan with the broth. Cover with aluminum foil. Bake at 350 for 40 minutes. Remove foil and continue Baking for 15 minutes longer.

6. Heat the tomato sauce.

7. Put 6 Tbs. of sauce on a plate with a pepper.

8. Serve with grated cheese.

MOMMY'S STUFFED CABBAGE

Stuffed Cabbage was another tasty dish of my mother Lucia's tasty repertoire, along with Stuffed Peppers, Braciole, Eggplant, Stuffed Artichokes, Meatloaf, and a few others. Hey, I never really thought about it before, but it seems my mom liked making a lot of dishes that were stuffed. Braciole are stuffed beef rolls, and of course the Peppers, Artichokes, and Cabbage. "Ripieno" is the Italian word for stuffed food. So stuffed cabbage in Italian is Cavalo Ripieno and Artichokes are Carciofi Ripieno. Make em, eat em, and enjoy, Mangia Bene!

INGREDIENTS:

1 medium onion, minced
3 cloves of garlic, minced
6 tablespoons chopped parsley
6 Tbs. bread crumbs
2 eggs, Salt & Pepper to taste
1 cup long grain rice, cooked
2 lb. ground beef
½ cup grated Pecorino Romano
1 medium Head Savoy Cabbage, about 2 lbs.
½ cup chicken broth
½ stick of Butter
¼ cup Olive Oil
2 cups tomato sauce

1. Cook rice according to directions on package, then let cool. You will end up with 2 cups rice.

2. Bring a large pot of salted water to the boil. Cut the bottom off of the cabbage. Cut the core out of the cabbage. Cook the cabbage in boiling water for 4-5 minutes, until the cabbage leaves are tender, yet still slightly firm. Drain cabbage and let cool.

3. In a large mixing bowl, add cooled rice, onion, garlic, parsley, ground beef, and breadcrumbs. Season the beef liberally with slat and pepper. Mix with hands.

4. Add cheese, a ½ a cup of the tomato sauce, and eggs. Mix thoroughly.

5. Take a small handful of the meat mixture and fill each cabbage leave. Place a small amount of the meat mixture about 3 inches from the end of a cabbage leave. Fold the end over the meat. Fold sides in, and then roll cabbage leave up to close. Roll cabbage leaves until all the meat mixture is gone.

6. Heat oven to 400 degrees. Coat a shallow glass or ceramic baking pan with the olive oil. Place half of the remaining tomato sauce into pan. Place all the rolled cabbages neatly into pan. Cover with remaining tomato sauce. Add chicken Broth and dot with butter on top.

7. Cook in oven at 400 degrees for 15 minutes. Lower heat to 350 and continue cooking for about 30 minutes until the meat inside the cabbage is fully cooked.

8. Take out of oven and let rest for 10 minutes before serving. Serve each person 3 or 4 Stuffed Cabbages with a little sauce. You may serve with roast or mashed potatoes or whatever you like. Buon Appetito!

CAPONATA

Caponata, one of Sicily's classic dishes, third in popularity after Cannoli and Pasta con Sarde (Pasta with Sardines). Caponata is a tasty dish of sweet and sour eggplant stew, that's quite versatile. It can be served on its own, on a sandwich, or with other items in a wonderful mixed antipasto.

Caponata makes a great accompaniment to any grilled meat, chicken, and especially fish and it is great to stuff into sandwiches.

Caponata like many other famous dishes will vary in taste from cook to cook. I have eaten it numerous times in Italy and New York and after trying many different versions, I've come up with my own famous recipe that is based on the one that my friend Gino makes. Gino C., who is originally from Siracusa in Sicily, and learned how to make Caponata from his father who was the original chef of their restaurant and is now retired.

Because of the content of salt, sugar, and vinegar, Caponata keeps well for up to two weeks and makes a great gift to any Italian food lover when it is presented in a nice mason jar. You can change this recipe to suit your own taste if you'd like, but it should always contain the eggplant and it should be sweet and sour (agro dolce).

The RECIPE

2 large eggplants, washed and cut into
¾" cubes, do not remove skin from eggplant
½ cup olive oil
3 medium onions, cut into ¼" dice
1 small Red Pepper and 1 Yellow Pepper
Cut into ½" dice
2 Celery stalks, ¼" dice
¼ raisons, soaked in hot water for 15 minutes
1 ½ cups Tomato Sauce
6 tablespoons sugar
6 tablespoons Balsamic vinegar
2 teaspoons salt, 3 teaspoons black pepper
3 tablespoons of capers

1. Sauté the peppers in a large pot with ½ of the olive oil for 10 minutes

2. Add the onions and sauté over low heat for 15 minutes.

3. Add the celery and tomato sauce and continue simmering. While the other ingredients are simmering, brown the Eggplant in several batches in a large frying pan with remaining olive oil. Add the browned Eggplant, sugar, and vinegar to the pot and simmer for 25 minutes over very low heat. Cool and serve on its own, as a topping for Crostini, as part of an Antipasto Misto, or as an accompaniment to any Grilled or Roast Fish, with Lamb, or with Grilled Chicken.

ITALIAN GREENS

If you don't already know, green vegetables are without a doubt the single best thing you can put in your body. Green vegetables and water, that is. Yes, you've gotta have water too.

Yes, green veggies are quite healthy. Italians love all sorts, other vegetables and fruits too. And they prepare their vegetables in a multitude of ways.

Italians, and especially Italian-Americans, love our green vegetables, and we really love greens, like; Broccoli Rabe (Rapini) and Escarole, or Scarola. Any green vegetables that are simply sautéed in garlic and olive oil are great favorites. Along with being immensely beneficial to good health, looking good, and tasting great, these sautéed greens are quick and easy to prepare.

Sautéed greens are the perfect accompaniment to any meat, fish, or poultry entrée and are great on their own or with other ingredients in an antipasto or as bruschetta on grilled or toasted Italian bread. You can prepare Broccoli Rabe, Escarole, Swiss Chard, Green Beans, Broccoli, Spinach, or Beet Greens all in this manner.

SCAROLA !

Escarole, in Italian the word is "*scarola*." In the Italian American dialect of my father's generation the word is usually pronounced,"Schka-role." Few are the young people these days that have ever even heard the word and I wonder how many have ever tasted this leafy green that many of us love so. "Schka-role" is of singular importance in the Italian-American cuisine. In the pantheon of Italian-American foods, escarole is way up there, along with Broccoli Rabe and Eggplant (melanzane). Escarole finds itself in soups, in recipes with beans and in stuffed versions, and sometimes on pizza.

In our family, my sister Barbara and I are the ones who love sautéed escarole most. It's simply sautéed with garlic, good olive oil, salt & pepper and "Basta," that's it, it's done and it's tasty as heck. This sautéed escarole is our favorite side-dish with roast chicken, pork chops, steak, and grilled fish.

One of the best uses ever for "Scarola" is in the whimsical Southern-Italian soup, Italian Wedding Soup with chicken broth, chicken, little meatballs and escarole, "It's just divine."

And did you know? "Scarola," is slang for "Money" in Italian, as in "That car cost a lot of "Schka-Role!"

SAUTÉED ESCAROLE

Ingredients:

2 heads escarole washed and roughly chopped
7 cloves garlic, peeled and sliced
¼ teaspoon crushed red pepper, ¼ cup olive oil

1. Blanch escarole in boiling salted water for 2 minutes. Drain off water. Drain again and squeeze excess water from Escarole.

2. Sauté garlic in oil until it just begins to brown.

3. Add red pepper and escarole. Sauté escarole over medium heat for about 6 minutes. Season with Salt and black pepper and serve.

GREEN BEANS

These Green Beans are cooked in the favorite Italian manner of cooking Green Vegetables, which is sautéed with garlic & Olive Oil. You can serve these beans as a side dish to any poultry, meat, or fish, or as a antipasto course. You can make a nice light meal with these beans by serving them over 2 Fired or Scrambled Eggs. Try it some time, it's real good, "e Tutto Bene."

INGREDIENTS:

1 ½ pounds fresh String Beans
5 Garlic Cloves, peeled and sliced thin
7 tablespoons Olive Oil
½ teaspoon Red Pepper Flakes
Salt & Black Pepper to taste

1. Cut off rough ends of string beans and any blemished pieces. Cook string beans in rapidly boiling salted water for 2 ½ minutes. Remove from heat and drain.

2. Add drained beans to a bowl of iced water to stop cooking. Let sit for 4 minutes, then drain dry.

3. Heat Olive Oil in a large frying pan. Add garlic and cook on low heat for 2 minutes. Add drained green beans and red pepper to pan. Cook on high heat for 5 minutes as you mix beans while cooking.

4. Season with Salt & Black Pepper to taste and serve.

BROCCOLI RABE
a.k.a. *Rapini*

Rapini is the Italian word what we Italian-Americans call Broccoli Rabe. Most of us just love it, and are sort of protective of it and proud that it is sort of our own. Well, yes in New York where I live and where the Italian-American enclave is quite strong, the bitter green vegetable of the broccoli family, Broccoli Rabe is much loved and well revered. We feel it is our own, as most of the rest of America and Americans don't really eat it all that much. Yes, there are a good amount of non-Italians in New York who eat it in restaurants, but it is really ours, an Italian-Thing as they say.

As has been said already, we love our greens, Italians do, and especially what in America are known as Italian Greens like Escarole and Broccoli Rabe, and of late, a wonderful wild salad green that is a favorite in Rome, the bitter but tasty Punterelle which you can get a wonderful salad of in season at the very popular Bar Pitti in my neighborhood of Greenwich Village, New York. Punterelle Salad is delicious with its classic anchovy dressing, the perfect foil for these crispy bitter greens.

Well, back to Broccoli Rabe, full of nutrition as any green vegetable are, Broccoli Rabe goes great with most meat, poultry, or fish dishes, especially any of these items that are grilled or simply roasted without any sauce.

Many might not know that Broccoli Rabe makes a great antipasto item, in the same way it is prepared for a side dish (Contorni), sautéed with Garlic and Olive Oil, you can have this Rapini as a nice little antipasto before the following courses. Broccoli Rabe is of course most famous as a contorni or side dish with your meal. It is also great on a sandwich of Roast Pork with Broccoli Rabe and shaved shards of Parmigiano Reggiano or Provolone, or as a Sausage & Broccoli Rabe Sandwich. And not many will know of another great dish that can be served as a antipasto or Secondo main-course dish, is Rapini sautéed with garlic and oil and topped with a grilled or sautéed link of Sweet or Hot Italian Sausage. For a antipasto you would give one piece of sausage on top of the Broccoli Rabe, and for a main course, 3 pieces of Sausages and you've got a nice easy meal that is fit for a King. What's better than that.

And let's not forget the famed southern Italian dish of Orecchiette with Sausage and Broccoli Rabe that's eaten all over the south of Italy, in; Campania, Calabria, Sicily, and Apulia as well.

SAUTEED BROCCOLI RABE And?

1 pound bunch of fresh Broccoli Rabe. Andy Boy brand is great.
2-3 cloves Garlic, peeled and coarsely chopped
7 tablespoons Italian Olive Oil
a pinch of Pepperoncino (Red Pepper Flakes)
Sea Salt & Black Pepper

1. Cut ends of Broccoli Rabe and any blemishes if there are any. Wash in cold running water. Cut Broccoli Rabe in to 2 or 3 pieces for each stem.

2. Bring a pot of water to the boil, and add one tablespoon salt.

3. Cook the Broccoli Rabe in rapidly boiling water for 3 minutes. Drain, and put the Broccoli Rabe under cold running water for 2 minutes. Drain.

3. Heat a large frying pan over medium heat. Add Olive Oil and Garlic. Cook garlic over medium heat 2 to 3 minutes until the garlic starts to get a little brown on the edges. Lower heat to very low, add Red Pepper. Cook 1 minute over low heat. Add the drained Broccoli Rabe and turn heat up to high. Cook over high heat for about 5 minutes, and serve immediately.

Note: As stated earlier, you can make a wonderful antipasto of this cooked Broccoli Rabe topped with 1 piece of cooked Italian Sweet or Hot Sausage on top. Serve 3 pieces with the Broccoli Rabe for a main course. Another wonderful item is a Rapini & Salsice Bruschetta. Break up 2 or 3 pieces of Italian Sweet or Hot Sausage and cook. Cut the Broccoli Rabe to smaller pieces and cook as in the above recipe. Add Sausage to Broccoli Rabe. Cut several pieces of Italian or French Bread into half inch slices and toast. Rub the toasted bread with a pieced of raw garlic (great flavor). Top each piece of toasted bread with some of the Sausage and Broccoli Rabe mixture and serve. Your guest will love it. And they'll love you too. "Bravo! See all you can do with Broccoli Rabe? You had know idea, did you?" Enjoy!

Yogi Berra

Yogi Berra was, along with Joe DiMaggio, and Phil Rizzutto one of major league baseball's great Italian American ball-players. Born in St. Louis, Yogi grew up in the Italian neighborhood called "The Hill," where he ate lots of; Sausages, Maccheroni, and other Italian Specialties made by Momma Berra.

Yogi has been loved by millions over the years, especially his Italian-American Brethren. Here are a few of his quotes we thought you might like. Enjoy!

"You better cut the Pizza in 4 pieces, cause I'm not hungry enough to eat six."

"Baseball is 90% mental, the other half is physical."

"A Nickel ain't worth a Dime any more."

"It's just like Deja-Vu all over again."

"It ain't over till it's over."

ITALIANS & EGGS

Not many would think of Italians as being big egg eaters, but if you thought that, you'd be wrong. Italians probably eat more eggs than Americans, and they certainly have more ways to prepare them, especially in the form of the marvelous Italian Frittata. Italians eat Hard-Boiled Stuffed Egg at Wine Bars all over Italy, and they eat all kinds of Frittati mostly for lunch, but for dinner with a salad or as a late night snack as well. The fillings for Frittata are endless, with spinach, spaghetti, potato, and mushroom being most common.

One famous Italian Egg dish is Uovo en Purgatorio, a dish of a couple eggs cooked in spicy tomato sauce and served over toasted Italian Bread. But when it comes to Italian-Americans vs. our Italian brethren in Italy, Italian-Americans eat quite a bit more eggs than Italians in Italy. Where Italian-Americans beat out Italians in Italy in egg consumption is in the area of Egg Sandwiches, of which we just love, and these are another of our little secrets. American's of other ethnic origins might not know of these tasty little sandwiches as we mostly eat them at home and the only Italian Egg Sandwich you are likely to see in an Italian-Deli is one of Sausage Pepper and Eggs. You're gonna have to go into a real heavy-duty Italian neighborhood in Philly, Chicago, Brooklyn, and other parts of New York to find one, and even then you're not gonna see many around.

My favorite Egg Sandwiches are the previously mention Sausage Pepper & Egg and one my dear Aunt Helen (born in Salerno) taught me way back when. It's a sandwich that's not that well known and is sort of a family secret. I've cooked it for my friends, who have all gone nuts for it, and love it so much that since we have a good number of dinner parties, my friends asked me to top crostini with this egg sandwich filling. Oh, "So what is it," you want to know? Well, it's quite simple, but supremely tasty. It's spinach sautéed with butter and olive oil then mixed in with eggs (Scrambling) and topped with the best quality grated Parmigiano Reggiano or Grana Padana Cheese. The result is amazing. One day I went over to Aunt Helen's house to pay a visit to her and my Uncle Frank. As always Aunt Helen asked me if I wanted to eat. Well, more of an order than a question. "Heck yeah," Aunt Helen, not what I said, but in my mind. OK, is what I said to Aunt Helen, one of the greatest Italian home-cooks this country has ever seen, her food was marvelous. Aunt Helen's Meatballs are my all-time favorites.

Anyway on this day, Aunt Helen gave me this sandwich. It was a Sandwich of Eggs scrambled with spinach and Parmigiano, and I was in love at first bite. Dam, this sandwich was a revelation. I asked Aunt Helen how she made it, she told me, and the rest is history. I made it for my friends who all went nuts for it as well, and I still make it to this very day, keeping my Aunt Helen's memory alive, I always think of her and that day whenever I make it, Panino di Uovo e Spinaci. Yumm! You just gotta try one.

So Frittata? They are quite a wonder this flat little Italian Omelette that can take on just about anything to go inside as a the filling. You can make them with an assortment of vegetables, with mushrooms, Spinach and Cheese, or my favorite, which I've never seen in Italy, I think I invented it, cause I've never seen anyone else make it, is Sausage & Peppers. Dam tasty.

Frittata are amazingly versatile. In Italy they are most often served thin and whole for most typically lunch, with maybe a little salad on the side. Over here, we Italian-Americans like to make them thicker and cut them into wedges to snack on, stuff in sandwiches, and bring along on a road-trip or in a picnic basket with Salami, Cheese, Bread and Wine. Now that's a good picnic basket.

FRITTATA

Frittata, they're quite a wonder. Italian Flat Omelets that are tasty, versatile and easy to make. I've been making them for years. They're one of my favorites. Frittata are quite versatile. You can fill them with a endless variety of ingredients, both fresh made or leftover, and this is one of the great uses and attributes of this Italian wonder, The Frittata. Americans are just recently learning about them. Italian Americans have known of, made, and have been eating Frittata in many forms for years. In the past several years you see them popping up in cafes, delis, and restaurants as the rest of American is now catching on to what Italian-Americans have known for years.

There are several different ways to eat and use Frittata. You can make a small one with two or three eggs and what ever filling you choose like Spinach and Parmigiano or Mushrooms and eat the whole Frittata for one person for lunch or dinner, with or without a green salad on the side.

The best and most useful use of Frittata is to make a large one using 8 to 12 eggs and whatever filling you choose. My favorites are Sausage & Pepper, Broccoli with Goat Cheese or Fontina, and the Spaghetti Frittata that has a cute little story behind it with me and my Aunt Fran. Anyway, when you make one of these large Frittata, the great thing is that you let it cool down, serve it at room temperature, cutting the frittata into wedges and eating it this way. A wedge of frittata can be an antipasto item on its own, part of a mixed antipasti misti, or my favorite, pulling a already made frittata out of the refrigerator and just cutting off a wedged shape piece and eating a piece any time day or night when you are hungry and need a little snack.

Frittata are great items to include in a picnic, at a barbecue, and are especially goo if you're on a long road trip in the car, in a bus, train, or plane, a piece or two of frittata is great to bring along. If you're on a plane, get hungry, and you have a wedge or two of frittata with you, you'll be happy as heck that you brought it along. Yes they make great travel food, The Frittata. They're also great as part of a buffet or to pass around little pieces as Hors D'Oeuvres at a cocktail   party

SAUSAGE & PEPPER FRITTATA

INGREDIENTS:

Olive Oil
8 Large Eggs, beaten and season with Salt & Pepper
4 links Italian Sweet Sausage
2 Red Bell Peppers, cleaned and cut in 1 inch strips
2 medium Onions, sliced in 1" slices
2 cloves garlic, peeled and sliced thin
1 bunch Italian Parsley, washed and chopped rough
half cup grated Parmigiano Reggiano or Grana

1. Place sausage in a small pot and cook in low simmering water for 10 minutes.

2. Remove sausages from water and cut in to 1" pieces.

3. Sauté sausages in a 10" non-stick pan with Olive Oil for about 6 minutes at medium heat until all surfaces of the sausage is nicely browned.

4. Remove sausage and keep on the side. Put the Bell Peppers in the same pan. Sauté over low heat for 10 minutes. Add onions and sauté for 8 minutes.

5. Add Sausages back to pan and continue cooking on low heat for 2 minutes. Add garlic and cook for 3 minutes.

6.   Beat eggs in a large bowl with salt and pepper. Add grated cheese and most of the chopped parsley, reserving some of the parsley to sprinkle over the finished Frittata.

7.   Turn the heat up high and cook for 1 minute. Add the eggs and cook while constantly mixing the eggs with other ingredients.

8.   When most of the eggs have cooked but there is still some uncooked eggs on top, take the pan off the heat. Let cool a few minutes. Take a plate that's larger than the diameter of the pan you're cooking in. Place the plate over the pan, then flip over so the uncooked part of the Eggs is on top of the plate.

9.   Add olive oil to pan and turn heat up high for 1 minute. Slide the frittata back in to the pan with the raw egg side of the frittata going in to the hot pan. Turn heat down to low and cook for about 2-3 minutes until the eggs are completely cooked through. Cut into wedges and serve hot, or put into a picnic basket or your lunch box and enjoy whenever.

Daniel Bellino-Zwicke

PASTA *"We Call It Maccheroni"*

So who doesn't love Pasta? Pasta? Some maybe? I've never met one. Pasta is loved the World over and no more than in the mother land of Italy, and in a land where millions of Italians left their country (Italy) for a better life in America. We all know, most Americans no matter if they're Italian, Polish-American, Irish, Latin, or wherever their family comes from, they Love Pasta. But no one loves Pasta like Italian-Americans. Some of us want it practically every day. We crave it, and when we do, that craving must be satisfied. I can remember many instances that rally amplify how much we love it. Two really stick out, and they both concern my cousin Joe, one of the all-time great fanatical *Pasta Lovers* if there ever was one. One of these two instances was when I was the Wine-Director at the 100 year-old plus Italian Restaurant, Barbetta on West 46th Street in New York. My cousin Joe and his wife Alexandra were having dinner at Barbetta one night. They had a little antipasto to start, and were having a nice "Combination Pasta Plate" of; homemade Angolotti alla Piedmontese, Gnocchi al Gorgonzola, and Tagliolini Pomodoro. My cousin Joe really loved that plate, and shyly asked if he could have another of the same plate, before his Bisteca Fiorentina came out. So I, along with the kitchen granted his wish. He had the second plate of pasta and loved it just as much as the first. However when his Steak came out, all he could eat of it, was 1 little bite. He was too full, yet perfectly satisfied as he had those 2 Tasty Plates of his beloved Pasta. That's pasta story # 1.

The second memorable instance of my cousin's love of pasta which illustrates not only his love of Italian Maccheroni, but also of most Italian-Americans, was one Sunday out on the East End of Long Island at Joe's house. That night we were all invited to his father's summer home on Long Island for a big Sunday meal. Joe's dad was making us a nice Seafood Dinner. Joe knew the menu and knew his father wasn't making any pasta, and Joe was having a strong craving for his favorite meal, Pasta, of any sort. Joe quietly asked me in a slightly embarrassed way if I could quick cook him up a plate of Spaghetti Pomodoro before we headed to his father's house even though we were going to have a huge meal over there. It didn't matter that his father was serving tasty Grilled Shrimp and Lobsters, there was nothing more Joe wanted than a nice plate of Pasta. He wasn't going to get it at his fathers, but he had to satisfy that strong crave, that of *Pasta*. Any Italian Maccheroni, even just a simple satisfying plate of Spaghetti Pomodoro, sprinkled with a tad of Sicilian Olive Oil and Parmigiano Reggiano. Well, it was me to the rescue. I made the pasta, Joe ate it, was completely satisfied and ready to go to dinner at dad's house, mission accomplished!

Yes we call it Macaroni after the Italian Maccheroni. We call it Macaroni and didn't really start calling it pasta till sometime in the early 80's. When I was a kid, it was Macaroni, and in those days we mostly at Spaghetti, Ziti, Stuffed Shells, Pastina, Ravioli, and Lasagna. And when I was a kid, it was always Ronzoni "Ronzoni Sono Buoni" the 1960's and 70's slogan and ad campaign for the Ronzoni Pasta Company of New York, that I remember so well. When I was a child, we didn't have DeCecco, Barilla, and all these other imported Italian brands of Macaroni. For us, it was always Ronzoni, and I still can remember my mother sending me to the Blue Goose Grocery Store or Belavia Italian Deli Groceria to get a box or two of Ronzoni # 9 Spaghetti. It was always # 9, Ronzoni Sono Buoni, "Ronzoni Is So Good."

Now, I must bring up a point. Along with the fact that, you don't have to be Italian or Italian-American to eat and love pasta, the fact is that not many people other than the Italians really know how to cook it that well. This is fact, though there are a few here and there who know how to make it well. Pretty much in order to make pasta well, you usually need an Italian. Hey, facts are facts.

Now a reason there are so many Italian Restaurants in this country is that most Americans dearly love Italian Food, and especially Pasta. One problem tough, they didn't grow up with it. Pasta! "It's not in their Blood," thus most can't make it well. Some may "think" they can and maybe some can, but not all that many. "Believe me." You have plenty of Italian Restaurants to get your fix of Baked Clams, Linguine Vongole (Clam Sauce), Lasagna, Chicken Parm, Veal Marsala, and whatever your heart desires in the way of Italian and Italian-American Food. Be careful though, unfortunately not every Italian restaurant is good, some might even be horrible, and not even run by Italians, which is a must. And yes, it's a sad fact that in many parts of the country where there aren't good sized Italian populations, the few restaurants they have what *they call Italian*, might very well be awful. They probably don't have any Pork Stores and not an Italian Pastry Shop in sight, and no Italian Caffe to get a properly pulled Espresso at. Oh, these poor people. They do have my sympathy. What's a person to do, they are not Italian, they can't cook Italian food well and there's not a good Italian restaurant in sight? Best thing to do is make friends with some Italians and get yourself invited to their house for dinner some time. The other thing to do, is make the recipes in this book, and practice, practice, practice, till you get it right.

Anyway, back to the Pasta, pasta in all its forms, the many shapes and sauces, and the wonder of it all. Myself, I was weaned on pasta, literally. Like many little toddlers now, millions before me and millions after, one of the things I was weaned on besides Gerber's Baby Food was a pasta called "Pastina," literal translation "Little Pasta" and that they are. Pastina are tiny little star shaped pasta that mamma gives to the little bambini. They are really tiny and easily go down a little baby's throat. Mamma coats the Pastina with a little knob of butter, the Pastina is yummy, and there you go, you're hooked on the stuff (Pastina and all Pasta) for the rest of your life. You love it, crave it, and want it all the time, for lunch, dinner, and a favorite Italian late night snack after a night out on the town, you crave a nice bowl of Spaghetti Aglio Olio. In Rome and other parts of Italy, Spaghetti Aglio e Olio it is a tradition after a night of a little drinking, to go back to someone's home (of the group of friends you're out with that night) and cook up a large bowl of Spaghetti Aglio e Olio for everyone to eat, similar to the tradition many Americans go to a Diner late at night after a night of imbibing in a bit of alcohol.

Spaghetti with Garlic and Oil is quite wonderful and one of most Italian-American's favorites. You will always have Olive Oil, Garlic, Spaghetti and other dry pasta on hand. If you don't have these items in your cupboard at *all times*, you're not a true Italian. Eat Spaghetti Aglio e Olio late night after a night on the town. Just like they do in Rome and all over Italy. If you happen to have some canned or jar of Anchovies on hand, all the better, Spaghetti with garlic, oil, and Anchovies, dam tasty, and so beautiful in its own simplistic way. Makes me think of one of the times Al Pacino was at Barbetta when I was working there. It wasn't on the menu, but that's what Al wanted, a simple plate of Spaghetti Aglio e Olio.

So right there, we've covered the two opposite spectrums of the Italian and Italian-American pasta experience, which is vast. On one end, there is "Pastina" the first pasta of so many thousands of plates of pasta you will have in your lifetime, and in so many different forms. You have your first pasta "Pastina" when you are a very small child, a baby. You grow up, you're an adult and out on the town. You've got the munchies, you're hungry, it is tradition to eat what? Right, Spaghetti with Garlic and Oil. Well yes, you might have a sandwich whatever. But you might not always have all the ingredients; bread, cheese, Prosciutto, ham, eggs whatever. If you're Italian, you always, but always have, red pepper flakes, Spaghetti, garlic, and olive on hand, and just for this reason, the Midnight Bowl of Spaghetti. Basta!

May I get back to the Pastina a moment, if you don't mind? Yes, as a baby and into young childhood my mother used to make Pastina for my brothers, sister, and myself. Coated with butter and sprinkled with Parmesan, we loved it so. Still do. My mother didn't make a lot of different pastas, but the few pastas we had, we had often. My mom's favorites, which became our favorites were, Lasagna (Mommy made a great one), Spaghetti & Meatballs, Ravioli, Baked Ziti, Stuffed Shells, and Rigatoni with the Sunday Sauce of; Meatballs, Sausages, and Braciole.

Ravioli was always a much loved treat in our household. My mother always bought a box each of Cheese and Meat Ravioli from a great Pasta Shop in Lodi, New Jersey that makes great home-made Ravioli, and other pastas, but they're most famous for the Ravioli. The place is Vitamia on Harrison Avenue in Lodi, and their Ravioli are superb. My mother would make a tomato sauce, cook up the Ravioli, and when we'd get them on the plate and sprinkle on a bit of Parmigiano Reggiano, we were in Heaven. And sprinkle on the Parmigiano, or should I say grate it on, for we didn't have that ugly green can of fake-parmesan, but the real thing, a chunk of Pecorino Romano or Parmigiano Reggiano from Parma, Italy. We had a metal box-grater for grating the cheese, and that's just what we did. As a little boy, before I was old enough to use it myself, I was always fascinated by that box-grater. It was a joy and wonder to me. Ah, the simple pleasures of life.

Pasta, you gotta have it, a fave of Italian-Americans in New York, New Jersey, and all across the land, whether it's a tasty bowl of Linguine Vongole (Clam Sauce), Fettuccine Bolognese, the beloved Sunday Sauce with Rigatoni, Ziti, or other short Maccheroni, or Mommy's Stuffed Shells, maybe a special treat of homemade Ravioli, or a simple plate of Spaghetti with Garlic & Oil the way Al Pacino likes. That's Pasta?

RONZONI SONO BUONI

"Ronzoni Sono Buoni," if you are Italian and grew up in the New York area in the great decades of the 1960's and or 70s, you know the slogan. We Italians do love our pasta, we're weaned on it! Pasta is the main staple of our diet. Many are fanatical about and love it so, and insist on having it several times a week. I'm one. Pasta, can be covered in a wide variety of sauces, in some soups like; Pasta Fagoli (Pasta Fazool), in Minestrone's, with Pasta and Peas, and Pasta con Ceci (Chick Peas). Yes, we are weaned on it. Mommy gave me, my bothers, and sister Pastina coated in a bit of butter and Parmigiano when we were just tod-dlers and every so often I have to pick up a box of Ronzoni Pastina, as I love and crave it still, and of late as with many my age, you start craving things you loved as a child, thus my stints with Pastina. "Ronzoni Sono Buoni," it means, Ronzoni is So Good, and that it is. This brand of Pasta, born in New York City at the turn of the century in 1915, and has been a mainstay of not only Italian-Americans of the East Coast but, for all. For years before the surge of many a imported pasta product in the U.S., Ronzoni, was not the only game in town for Macaroni, there was the Prince and Creamette, as well, but Ronzoni dominated the market, and though I don't have stats, I would wager to say that 85 to 90 % of all commercial pasta sold in the New York, New Jersey, and Philadelphia areas was Ronzoni, the pasta in the bright blue boxes, Ronzoni Sono Buoni. God I wonder how many plates and bowl of Spaghetti, Ziti and other Ronzoni pastas I ate over the years, starting with Pastina as a toddler and moving to Spaghetti with Tomato Sauce and or Meatballs, Baked Ziti, Stuffed Shells and more. Oh "Stuffed Shells," they bring back memories of my mother. Stuffed Shells were one of her favorites. Yes, we had them often, along with Lasagna made of course with Ronzoni Lasagna. You don't see Stuffed Shells around that much any more, they used to be on many a restaurant and even more home menus. There popularity has waned, but every once and a while I'll pick up a box of Ronzoni large shells, just for the purpose of bringing back those memories of mom making them and me loving them as a child. I'll make a batch of tomato sauce, cook the Ronzoni Shells, and stuff them with ricotta and Parmigiano, sprinkle on a bit of Mozzarella, bake them in tomato sauce, and "Voila" Stuffed Shells of days gone by. I do the same with a Pastina as I still love the dish so, dressed with butter and fresh grated Parmigiano Reggiano, it makes me feel like a kid again! Yum, delicious little pleasure you can whip up in minutes and bring back visions of your youth. All with some butter, Parmigiano and a box of Ronzoni Pastina. That's Ronzoni, every bit a part of my life and youth as a spring ol Slinky, Etch-A-Sketch, The Three Stooges, Saturday Morning Cartoons, and all the favorites of my youth, Ronzoni Sono Buoni, "Ronzoni it's so good!"

ME and MY PASTINA

Pastina? This is where my Pasta eating days began, way back when? Yes, Pastina is the first pasta I ever ate. The first of many a fine pasta that I came to love, me and millions other little Italian babies, Italian and Italian-American. It's already been stated, we're weaned on the stuff. Pastina that is!

What's Pastina you say? Well, first off, Pastina is what the Italian name implies "Little Pasta." Pastina are tiny little star shaped pasta, very tiny, and this is why they are first given to babies being weaned off mothers-milk. Mama cooks these tiny little star shaped pasta, adds a little butter, lets them cool down a little as not to burn the mouth of the little bambini.

Pastina in Butter, "it's love at first bite," Yum! When you get a little older, mamma adds a little grated Parmigiano Reggiano, it's sublime. You can even have Pastina as a dessert simply drizzling a little Honey over the Pastina with butter, and a little dollop of Ricotta on top of the buttered pastina and a drizzle of honey to complete the trick. Yum, I can taste it now.

Yes, Pastina, I love it so. Reminds me of my childhood, and "That's a Good Thing."

TOMATO SAUCE

Ok, now whatever you call it; *Sauce*, Salsa di Pomodoro, Sugo di Pomodoro, or Tomato Sauce, it's just that *Tomato Sauce.* So here we go. Without question Italian Food is the undisputed King of Ethnic Foods in America. Yes we love Chinese Food, which runs second to Italian, and Mexican, French, Thai, and all the rest, but Italian is King. What are the most popular foods consumed in America? I'd have to say; Burgers, Pizza, Pasta, and Sandwiches are in the lead as concerning dishes eaten most by Americans. Spaghetti with Tomato Sauce is in the top ten. Unfortunately, a lot of it is not very good. We're talking about jar-sauce here, something *"no self-respecting Italian ever eats."* You can actually say, when people eat Spaghetti in this manner, with not-very-authentic jarred tomato sauce. This so-called sauce (the Jar Kind) is not Italian or even Italian-American, it's *American*, and *bad American food* at that. "Please "Please" don't associate it with Italian-America and the fine food we eat, "please don't!" So if you eat over-cooked spaghetti with massed produced commercial Tomato Sauce from a jar or can, "you are not eating Italian," *nor Italian-American*, but American home-convenience food, that's quick, easy, econ-omical to make, and not very good to eat. Well we don't think so (Italian-Americans). We eat the real thing. So, that jar-stuff and the over-cooked past, please, don't call that kind of pasta, Italian, "It's Not," it's

American, OK? Got That? Basta!

When we talk about Tomato Sauce (Salsa Pomodoro) we're talking about fresh made tomato sauce, made with tomatoes, olive oil, fresh Garlic, Pepperoncino, and fresh Basil, cooked at home by you or some family member. And when I say fresh, that doesn't mean that the tomatoes have to be fresh tomatoes, which are only in season about 8 weeks a year. The rest of the year fresh tomatoes are inferior to the great product of canned tomatoes, or jarred Passata di Pomodoro (Italian Tomato Puree in jars). Cans of San Marzano Tomatoes from the environs of Naples, Italy or tomatoes from your garden are best. Also, there are many great brands of tomatoes canned in the U.S.A. . One of the best ways of all to make a good homemade tomato sauce at home is if you have your own homemade Passata di Pomodoro from tomatoes grown in your own garden to full ripeness, or Passata that you made from fresh tomatoes that you bought in bulk at a inexpensive price when tomatoes are at the peak of the season. Many Italian-Americans make Passata di Pomodoro (Tomato Puree) from tomatoes they have grown in their backyard and picked at the height of perfect ripeness perfection. Some, if they don't grow them will buy fresh tomatoes in bulk in season (at a low case price) and make the passata and some make the passata with a combination of tomatoes they grew in the garden, and along with a box or bushel of fresh tomatoes from a farm, farmers market, or wholesaler. This practice of growing your own tomatoes and canning them (actually in Glass Jars) is one of Italian-America's great time-honored traditions, which many families still do to this day, along with another wonderful Italian-American Family Ritual of making your own homemade wine. But don't fret if your family doesn't do this, you can make some great sauce with many of the fine canned and jarred tomato products from America or imported from Italy.

Tomato Sauce is quite a wonderful thing. You can do many things with it; top a Frittata with it, for a Fritatta di Pomodoro e Parmigiano and you've got a tasty little meal. You need a cup or so of tomato sauce to make Caponata and to add to many Italian recipes. When you have a Tomato Sauce already made, you can make many other Pasta Sauces simply by adding different ingredients. You can make Pasta with Zucchini or Cucuzza (Googootz) by simply sauté some Zucchini or Cucuzza (Large Italian Squash) in olive oil with garlic, salt, and pepper, adding tomato sauce and you have a couple new sauces right there. Sauté some Mushrooms, add tomato sauce and you can make Spaghetti con Funghi. To make the famous Sicilian dish Pasta alla Norma you sauté Eggplant in olive oil with garlic, add "You guessed it," tomato sauce, cook your pasta of choice, toss it with the Eggplant and Tomato Sauce, grate some Ricotta Salata over the top, and you've got a classic plate of Pasta alla Norma. All these tasty dishes because you've learned how to make Tomato Sauce. Get my drift? "Capece?" And that's not all. When you have some tomato sauce on hand, you have the base for such wonderful dishes as; Eggplant Parmigiano, Veal Parm, or Chicken Parmigiano. You've got your tomato-sauce, all you have to do is get some Mozzarella, Parmigiano, and boneless chicken breast. Bread and fry the chicken breast, put in a pan covered with some tomato sauce, a sprinkle of grated Parmigiano, top with Mozzarella, and bake in the oven, and Voila, you've got Chicken Parm, one of Italian-America's and all Americans favorite dishes of all. "You've got Tomato Sauce. The World Is Yours!"

TOMATO SAUCE RECIPE

INGREDIENTS:

3-28 oz. cans San Marzano crushed tomatoes
or other good quality Italian style tomatoes
7 cloves minced garlic
1 small onion, minced
½ teaspoon crushed red pepper
¼ cup virgin olive oil
¼ cup chopped fresh basil or 1 teaspoon dried
Salt and pepper to taste

1. In a 6 quart or larger pot, sauté onions over a low flame for 3 minutes. Add garlic and cook for 3-4 minutes. Do not let the garlic get dark or burn.

2. Add tomatoes, turn heat up to high and stir. When sauce starts to bubble, turn flame down so the sauce is at a low simmer. Simmer for 45 minutes while frequently stirring the bottom of the pan to keep sauce from burning. Add fresh basil in the last ten minutes of cooking.

3. Cook whatever pasta you choose (spaghetti is best) according to directions on package. Drain pasta, toss with tomato sauce and a drizzle of olive oil, plate, and serve with cheese.

SPAGHETTI POMODORO
"with Tomato Sauce"

Spaghetti Pomodoro, Spaghetti Tomato Sauce, a dish eaten a million times every day in America, but fewer times is it done right. Yes, Spaghetti With Tomato Sauce is an American favorite. Oh, but what *horrors* of the *real thing* are served up millions of times each and every day in America. People serve Spaghetti with all kinds of awful jarred and even canned, so-called tomato sauce, "Yuk!" Well, that's another thing, it's American Spaghetti with Tomato Sauce, and should be separated from the "real thing," and that's Spaghetti Pomodoro served by Italians in Italy or good Italian-American cooks in America. Italian-Americans who make Tomato Sauce in the correct manner, served up with perfectly cooked Spaghetti al Dente, a bit of good Italian Olive Oil drizzled over the top, and fresh grated Pecorino Romano or Parmigiano Cheese. We'll tell you the right way, and it's up to you if you do it right, to give the dish the respect it deserves, as a proper plate of Spaghetti Pomodoro.

HOW TO MAKE IT?
SPAGHETTI POMODORO

1 pound Imported Italian Spaghetti
3 cups Tomato Sauce, recipe page
Grated Parmigiano Reggiano or Pecorino Romano
Olive Oil & Salt

To make a great plate of Spaghetti Pomodoro follow these directions.

1. Bring a large pot of salted water to the boil.

2. Heat the Tomato Sauce in a separate pot or pan.

3. Put the Spaghetti into the pot with rapidly boiling water and cook according to directions on package. Start testing the doneness of the spaghetti 1 ½ to 2 minutes before the cooking time on package. You do this by pulling a strand of spaghetti out of the pot and biting into it to test the doneness.

4. When the spaghetti is done, drain it into a colander, reserving a bit of the pasta cooking water.

5. Put pasta back in pot it cooked in. Add a few drops of olive oil and mix. Add half the tomato sauce and mix.

6. Plate Spaghetti equally amongst 4 plates. Top each plate with an equal portion of remaining sauce. Pass the grated cheese and enjoy a perfect plate of Spaghetti Pomodoro

BAKED ZITI

When I was growing up in New Jersey a few years back, Baked Ziti was quite the popular dish. We ate it at home and many a large family gathering, like a Baby's Christening, Engagement Party, or some other sort of large family function, Baked Ziti was a mainstay. Baked Ziti was big in Jersey, Brooklyn, Boston, New York, and I guess all of Italian-America. Its popularity has diminished over the years; probably do to the fact that some delis that might have used it as a catering item didn't always do such a good job. We never had that problem as we always had Aunt Fran, Uncle Tony, or Aunt Helen make ours. Although I was at some parties that had the food catered and the ziti may not have been up-to-snuff. Whatever, when it's done right, baked Ziti is tasty, it's easy to make, and great to make ahead, heat up and serve for easy party planning. Yes Baked Ziti is not quite as popular as it once was, never the less, as a result of its once huge popularity, it still lingers on and many still love. Especially old-timers. Here's a good recipe below, that when made correctly, it's sure to please.

RECIPE: BAKED ZITI

2 pounds Ziti (Ronzoni or other brand)
2 pounds low moisture Mozzarella, cubed or shredded
2 lbs. Ricotta Cheese
2 cups grated Parmigiano Reggiano or Pecorino Romano Cheese of best quality
10 cups Tomato Sauce from previous recipe of Tomato Sauce

PREPARATION:

1. Preheat oven to 400 degrees. Bring a large pot of salted water to the boil.

2. Heat the Tomato Sauce over a medium flame for 10 minutes.

3. Add ziti to boiling water and cook for about 10 minutes until slightly al dente. Remove ziti from heat and drain in a colander.

4. Get a baking pan that is large enough to hold all the ziti. Coat pan with a thin film of olive oil, then coat bottom of pan with tomato sauce.

5. Put Ziti back in the pot it cooked in and add about 4 table spoons of olive oil and mix. Add 4 cups of tomato sauce to the ziti. Mix Ziti with tomato sauce. Add half the Ricotta Cheese and mix.

6. Place half the Ziti into your baking pan and spread out evenly. Spread 2 cups of the tomato sauce over Ziti. Cover the ziti with half the Mozzarella. Add remaining Ricotta and spread as evenly as possible over the Ziti. Sprinkle half the grated Parmigiano or Pecorino Romano over the Mozzarella and Ziti.

7. Add remaining Ziti to pan and repeat, covering the Ziti with 2 cups of tomato sauce, then the remaining Mozzarella, and ¾ cup of Grated Cheese, leaving some grated cheese for passing around the table once the Ziti is served.

8. Place pan of Ziti in oven and bake for 15 minutes at 400 degrees. Turn oven down to 350 degrees and bake for 20 minutes more. Remove Ziti from oven and let it rest for 8-10 minutes before serving.

9. Five minutes before you remove the Ziti from the oven, heat your remaining tomato sauce over low heat.

10. Serve each guest a good sized portion of Ziti. Dollop each plate of Ziti with a bit of tomato sauce and sprinkle on some Parmigiano or Pecorino Romano, whichever one you decide to use. Serve your guest and enjoy, Buon Appetito!

A Simple *"I Love You"* Means more than Money.

Frank Sinatra

MARINARA

What is Marinara Sauce? That's a good one. And I can tell you there is no one single definitive answer. Doesn't exists, unlike, Amatriciana or Bolognese Sauce, which both can have variations, they are still both pretty defined and the variations come after what defines a Bolognese or Amatriciana Sauce.

Well, one thing that a Marinara Sauce is, it's a Tomato Sauce, a type of Tomato Sauce and a Marinara Sauce will vary according to who makes it.

Italians (in Italy) refer to Marinara not as a Sauce but in association with a recipe as in Spaghetti al Marinara, this translates to Mariner's Spaghetti or in the style of the mariner, or "Sailor," and is of Southern Italy and Naples in particular. Southern Italian Spaghetti al Marinara does not contain any Seafood as some might think, and the name leads to imply.

Folklore has it that, Italian Sailors developed Marinara Sauce to cook on ships, as the high-acid content in tomatoes helped to preserve it well. Another theory is that the wives of Neapolitan Sailors cooked Spaghetti al Marinara for their husbands when they returned from sea.

So what is Marinara Sauce? Renowned Cookbook author and Restaurateur Lidia Bastianich says of marinara sauce, "The difference between marinara sauce and tomato sauce is this: Marinara is a quick sauce, seasoned only with garlic, pepper, and, if you like, basil or oregano. The pieces of tomato are left chunky, and the texture of the finished sauce is fairly loose. Tomato sauce, on the other hand, is a more complex affair, starting with puréed tomatoes and seasoned with onion, carrot, celery, and bay leaf, and left to simmer until thickened and rich in flavor." This is Lidia's version, but you'll see the one most often made in Italian Restaurants differ a bit from Lidia's.

Marinara Sauce is widely used in Italian-American Cuisine, and the sauce can vary from person to person and, cook-to-cook, chef-to-chef, restaurant to restaurant, "there is no one single exacting specific recipe, but all usually have Olive Oil, Garlic, Tomato, Pepperoncino, and Basil and or Oregano. Oregano seems to be the biggest single factor in what a Marinara Sauce actually is, as many versions of Marinara Sauce seem to have Oregano included in it, which is not usually present in true Italian (of and from Italy) Tomato Sauce, or Sugo al Pomodoro. One other factor, is that Marinara Sauce is cooked quickly, in about 10-15 minutes as opposed to 45 minutes or longer for regular Tomato Sauce.

OK, now, my Marinara Sauce, what I think it is, and how I make it. It's also how, not everyone but many others make it as well. Remember, I am of Italian-American ancestry; I cooked professionally for 20 years, in French, then Italian Restaurants. To me, the way I was taught and what I think is the best tasting Marinara Sauce of all, is as follows. To make Marinara Sauce, I already have my base, regular Tomato Sauce that I have made previously. When I was cooking in a restaurant and someone wanted Marinara Sauce, this is the one we made. We'd use about a cup and a half of our regular tomato sauce that was always on hand. When we got an order for Spaghetti Marinara, we'd put some Olive Oil and a single serving pan. Heat it, adding a good amount of chopped fresh Garlic. Cook the garlic, add a bit of Pepperoncino (Red Pepper Flakes) and a little dried Oregano. This was our flavoring base, and would considerably add much flavor to the base Tomato Sauce, making for an extremely tasty Marinara. Once the garlic has cooked to where it just starts to brown a bit, you add the Tomato Sauce and heat through. Once your spaghetti has finished cooking, you drain it, drop it in the pan with your Marinara Sauce, adding a bit of the pasta cooking water, toss the pasta, mix and serve. Voila, Spaghetti Marinara, my version and the one most accepted as Marinara when ordered at an Italian Restaurant in New York. Though there are others, this is not the defining Marinara Sauce Recipe, but I believe the one most widely used, and no matter, I can tell you it's dam tasty and, I always get raves whenever I make it.

So in the end, what is marinara? As I've said there is no one right singular answer, or description. But if you ask me and most any renowned Italian-American home cook or respected cooks and chefs in New York Italian Restaurants, they'll tell you the one I describe as what I call Marinara Sauce is the one most excepted. Marinara Sauce is Tomato Sauce that has already been made, then it's reheated and cooked in a pan that has a highly flavorful base of olive oil cooked while a good amount of garlic and a few flakes of Pepperoncini (Red Pepper flakes), add already cooked cooled tomato sauce to the pan with the garlic and olive oil, and possibly oregano, heat this and you have Marinara Sauce! Basta!

"New Jersey has the Best Tomatoes in The World."

LUCIANO PAVAROTTI

MARINARA SAUCE RECIPE

Ingredients:

1 & ½ cups Home-Made Tomato Sauce
5 tablespoons olive oil
1 or 2 cloves Garlic, peeled and chopped fine
Pepperoncino (Red Pepper flakes), 1/8 of a teaspoon
Oregano is "Optional" ¼ to ½ teaspoon if you use it

1. Heat olive oil with garlic over medium flame for 2 minutes.

2. Add Pepperoncino and Oregano if you are using it and cook 1 minute.

3. Add homemade Sugo di Pomodoro (Tomato Sauce)
that you cooked previously. Cook over medium heat for 3-4 minutes.

NOTE: This is enough Marinara Sauce for one portion of Marinara Sauce. To make for 4 people, increase ingredients by 4 times or whatever amount of servings you'd like.

SECRET SAUCE
"SEGRETO"

Tagliolini w/ Salsa Segreto. Secret Sauce? Shhhh!!! We lost our beloved Old-School Italian Red-Sauce Joint Gino's of Lexington Avenue a couple years back. Gino's opened in 1945 by Neapolitan Immigrant Gino Circicello, was a Gem of a Restaurant loved by its many loyal customers who kept the place packed and vibrant night-after-night, year-after-year. The place was perfect; Great Food and good wine at reasonable prices coupled with excellent service by friendly attentive waiters inside a homey comfy dining-room that everyone loved, from its cozy little Bar at the front of the restaurant, its Phone Booth (one of the last surviving in New York), and the famed Scalamandre Zebra Wallpaper that is as much a part of Gino's as the tenured old waiters, the Phone Booth, and the popular Chicken Parmigiano.

Among all the tasty pasta dishes, the Pasta with Salsa Segreta, (Segreto) "The Secret Sauce," was a perennial favorite at Gino's. All of Gino's legendary clientele loved it. Some of the clients just happened to be, people like; Frank Sinatra, Tony Bennett, and Joe DiMaggio, to name a few of a large string of luminaries to grace Gino's over the years. Gino's had many wonderful dishes that were soul satisfy, unpretentious, and tasty as heck. They were all of the usual suspects of typical Italian Red-Sauce Joints everywhere; from Baked Clams Oreganata, to

Shrimp Cocktail, to Spaghetti with Clam Sauce, Lasagna, the famed Veal Pamigiano, "the entire menu." I used to go to Gino's with my cousin Joe quite a bit. My sister Barbara came a couple times, as did my brother Michael. But it was usually me and Cousin Joe, and if anyone else was tagging along as well. Now I love my pasta as all good Italian-Americans do, but my cousin Joe? He had me beat. The guy loves his pasta, and wanted it practically every day. We tried the Salsa Segreta (Secret Sauce) on our very first trip to the marvelous Gino's Restorante. I think we had it with Tagliolini, but you can have it with Spaghetti, Rigatoni or whichever pasta you like. Well we loved the Salsa Segrete from the very first, and would get it every time we went. Often we'd get Baked Clams and Shrimp Cocktail to start, followed by a Half Portion each of Tagliolini with Salsa Segreto (Segrete), and as our main we might split a Veal Milanese with a "Nice Bottle of Chianti." We'd finish the meal with Espresso and a couple of Desserts, maybe a Tiramisu and a Chocolate Tartufo.

So the Secret Sauce, what's in it, you want to know? Yes I identified the Secret ingredients one day, I made it, and it tastes exactly the same, and that's as tasty as can possibly be, a 10 out of 10, you can't get any better. It's quite simple and you'd be amazed, but that's the essence of all Italian Cooking, simply tasty. The Secret of The Secret Sauce is, "I shouldn't tell you but I will." I should be charging you $100 just for this one recipe but I won't. "I hope you know what a bargain you people are all getting; my Sunday Sauce, Clemenza's Sunday Sauce, my

Lentil Soup recipe, Marinara Sauce, my *famed* Bolognese and more. I'm getting robbed here!" But here you go, The Secret-Ingredients in the Secret Sauce from the former Gino's Restaurant on Lexington Avenue across from Bloomingdales are *Butter* and *Parmigiano Reggiano Cheese* added to a simple tomato sauce as you toss the pasta (your Choice) with the Sauce. Basta! That's it! The Cat is out of the Bag. Enjoy! Are you Happy? "You better be!"

SALSA SEGRETO
"The SECRET SAUCE"

THE SECRET RECIPE! Ssshhhhhhs !!!!

The Ingredients: "That's The SECRET"

1-28 oz. cans San Marzano TomatoePassata or other
good quality crushed tomatoes
2 cloves minced garlic
1 small onion, minced
1/8 teaspoon crushed red pepper
5 tablespoons cup virgin olive oil
¼ cup chopped fresh basil or 1 teaspoon dried
Salt and pepper to taste
½ Stick Sweet Cream Butter or Lightly Salted
½ cup grated Parmigiano Reggiano Cheese

1. Make Tomato Sauce

2. In a 6 quart or larger pot, sauté onions over a low
flame for 3 minutes. Add garlic and cook for 3-4
minutes. Do not let the garlic get dark or burn.

3. Add tomatoes, turn heat up to high and stir. When
sauce starts to bubble, turn flame down so the sauce
is at a low simmer. Simmer for 45 minutes while
frequently stirring the bottom of the pan to keep
sauce from burning. Add fresh basil in at the last ten
minutes of cooking.

4. Cook whatever pasta you choose (spaghetti is best) according to directions on package. Drain pasta, toss with tomato sauce and a drizzle of olive oil, plate, and serve with Cheese.

5. Cook a pound of Pasta of your choice for 4 people, if just 2 people than cook a half pound of pasta, and cut the amount of Butter and Grated Parmigiano Cheese by half. Cook pasta according to directions on package. If using fresh Tagliolini or Fettuccine, the pasta will be cooked in 3-4 minutes.

6. Drain the pasta. Add to tomato sauce. Turn off heat. Add Butter and mix. Add grated cheese and mix. Serve the Pasta. Pass more grated Parmigiano to top the pasta with, eat and enjoy, "I guarantee you will."

ALFREDO

In the 60's and 1970's Fettuccine Alfredo was one of the great favorite dishes on Italian restaurant menus throughout the country. It was in the late 80's that the popularity of the dish started to wane for a couple of reasons, one being the Genesis of the health movement in The United States and reason two being the start towards more authentic Italian dishes and the almost total disdain (at the time) of the so-called cliché dishes, Fettuccine Alfredo being one of them.

To this day in 2013, being in the restaurant business, I still have people request this dish to me several times a week. Let me tell you, "this is the sign of a great dish, regardless of what anyone thinks otherwise." Fettuccine is quick and easy to make. Once you know how to make the sauce, you will be able to make a number of other dishes simply by changing or adding different ingredients.

You can make Tortellini Panna by substituting tortellini for the fettuccine, add a few cooked vegetables like mushrooms, peas, carrots, and broccoli florets and you have another hugely famous dish of the 70's and 80's, "Pasta Primavera", invented by none other then Siro Maccioni at Le Cirque. The dish still a popular dish there to this very day. Pasta Primavera is not on the menu and you have to be an insider to order it. When I was a Sous Chef at Caio Bella Restaurant, one of the hot trendy restaurants of the late 80's, I used to make a dish called Fettuccine al Lemone that only the regulars knew about. It was not on the menu, but if you were in-the-know you could get it. I used to make this dish for a rich Oil Baron's daughter from Kuwait and you can make it too simply by adding the zest from a couple lemons to the basic Fettuccine Alfredo recipe, and a few leaves of Fresh Basil is nice addition as well. That's Alfredo, Lemone, or Primavera, so please, Buon Appetito and enjoy.

Recipe for FETTUCCINE ALFREDO

1 lb. fresh Fettuccine
1 pt. heavy cream, ½ stick butter
1 cup grated Parmigiano
2 egg yolks, salt & pepper

1. Put the cream in a large frying pan. Bring to the boil, lower the flame and let the cream cook. Season the cream with salt and pepper to taste. Reduce volume by One-Third, this will thicken the sauce.

2. Cook the fettuccine and drain it. Put the fettuccine in to the pan with the cream. Add butter and stir.

3. Turn the flame off. Add egg yolks and Parmigiano and stir. Serve and pass around extra Parmigiano.

Note: You can make *Fettuccine Lemone* by adding the zest of two lemons to this recipe. Fresh basil is also another nice addition for the Lemone Sauce.

Daniel Bellino-Zwicke

SPAGHETTI with BROCCOLI

This is a dish similar to a Southern Italian favorite Broccoli Rabe and Pasta. This dish is made with regular Broccoli rather than the bitter Rapini (Broccoli Rabe). It is fast and easy to make. On top of that it's really tasty and quite healthy. I once made it for my friend Jimmy and his girlfriend. Jimmy loved it so much, I taught him how to make it, and he makes it at least once every week, sometimes twice. It's just that the dish is tasty, inexpensive, healthy, and quick and easy to cook.

2 heads fresh Broccoli. 6 cloves thinly sliced garlic
¼ cup olive oil, ¼ teaspoon crushed red pepper
1 ½ lbs. good quality imported Italian spaghetti
¼ cup grated Parmigiano Reggiano
1/3 stick of butter

Preparation:

1. Wash broccoli and cut into florets. Blanch Broccoli in boiling salted for 3 minutes.

2. Drain broccoli in a strainer. Place olive oil and garlic in a large frying pan. Sauté over low heat until the garlic just start browning. Add broccoli and sauté over medium heat for about 6 minutes.

3. While the broccoli is sautéing, cook spaghetti in a large pot of water according to directions on the Pasta package.

4. Drain spaghetti and add to pan with Broccoli. Add butter and toss. Plate Spaghetti with Broccoli and pass around the Grated Cheese.

NOTE: A variation on this dish is to add 1 cup of cooked Tomato Sauce to the spaghetti after draining it from the water. Plate the Spaghetti into six plates or pasta bowls, divide the sautéed broccoli evenly on top of each portion of Spaghetti and serve.

ORECCHIETTE
con SALSICE e RAPINI

Orecchiette w/Sausage & Broccoli Rabe

This is a real Southern Italian dish popular in Calabria, Puglia, and Campania, and a favorite Italian-Americans whose families hale from the south as well. The Sausage is tasty and very healthy. Gotta get your greens.

INGREDIENTS:

1 lb. Imported Italian Orecchiette
4 links Hot or Sweet Italian Sausage
1 lb. fresh Broccoli Rabe washed and cut into
1 ½" pieces
¼ cup Olive Oil
¼ teaspoon Hot Red Pepper flakes
1/3 cup grated Pecorino, salt and Black Pepper
4 cloves Garlic peeled and coarsely chopped
1/8 teaspoon Crushed red Pepper Flakes

Preparation:

1. Fill a large pot with 6-7 qts. Water and bring to boil. Add 3 tablespoons salt to water, then add Broccoli Rabe, cover pot and boil for three minutes.

2. Remove the broccoli Rabe with a slotted spoon from water and keep on the side.

3. Place 3 tablespoons olive oil in a large skillet. Add the Sausage and cook over medium heat until the sausage is completely cooked through. As the sausage is cooking, break the sausage with a wooden spoon into pieces that are about a inch-and-a-half around.

4. Cook Orecchiette in a large part of boiling that are about a inch-and-a-half around.

5. After the sausage has been cooked through, remove sausage from pan with a slotted spoon and set aside. Add the garlic to pan and a little more olive oil, if needed. Add Pepperoncino. Sauté the garlic over medium heat for about two minutes, then add the Broccoli Rabe and sauté for about five minutes over low to medium to heat. Season with Salt & Black Pepper to taste.

6. Drain cooked Orecchiette from water, reserving 3 tablespoons of water to toss with pasta. Add drained orecchiette and water to pan with Broccoli Rabe. Add sausage, toss and cook over medium heat for two minutes.

7. Serve 4-6 equal portions on plates or in pasta bowls. Sprinkle olive oil and grated Pecorino over Orechiette.
Serve and enjoy.

SCHIAVELLI PASTA

This is my version of Vincent Schiavelli's Pasta cu Vraccula Arriminatu (pasta with cauliflower) that my close Neapolitan friend Ada loves so much. Vincent includes anchovies and saffron, which Ada does not like so I have altered the recipe to suit her taste. I love Vincent's recipe with the anchovies and saffron but this is just another version and it should illustrate to people that recipes in cookbooks do not have to be followed to the letter and you can change them around, because you may not have all the ingredients available or simply to comply with your own taste. So remember you can always experiment with recipes. Have fun, and explore.

SCHIAVELLI PASTA

1 large head cauliflower, core and cut into
1-1/2" pieces
10 cloves of garlic, peeled
2-28 oz. cans crushed San Marzano Tomato's
1 medium onion, minced
½ teaspoon crushed red pepper
¼ cup olive oil, salt and pepper to taste

1. Place half the oil in a large pot with the minced onions. Sauté for three minutes. Add five cloves of garlic that have been thinly sliced. Sauté for 3 minutes over low heat. Add Red Pepper, sauté for 2 minutes.

2. Add tomatoes and simmer over low heat for 45 minutes.

3. While tomato sauce is simmering, place remainder of olive oil in a large frying pan and sauté the cauliflower over medium heat for 12-15 minutes until it is slightly browned.

4. Add remaining 5 whole garlic cloves with cauliflower. Sauté for about 5 minutes. Add salt and pepper to taste.

5. Add cauliflower to tomato sauce and cook for 10 minutes.

6. You can use almost any pasta for this sauce, although short pasta such as rigatoni, Ditalini, Orechietti, or Cavatappi work best.

7. Cook the pasta according to directions on package, drain, pour sauce over pasta and mix.

8. Serve with grated Pecorino Romano or Parmigiano Reggiano.

NOTE: If you'd like to use anchovies and saffron like Vincent does, you can add a pinch of saffron and three minced anchovy filets at step number (4), sauté' for two minutes. Continue to #

AMATRICIANA

This tasty sauce made with guanciale originates from Amatrice but is most famous in Rome where it is found on menus all over the city. The meat used in the sauce in Italy is Guanciale or Pancetta (un-smoked bacon). In my recipe I use a combination of pancetta and smoked bacon. I once had two Gentlemen from Lazio at my former restaurant Bar Cichetti order the Rigatoni Amatriciana that I had made for a special one night. They were flabbergasted that it was so good. They really couldn't believe an American could make their native dish taste so delicious. I couldn't believe it when they showed up the very next night to eat the Amatriciana again. After the meal they told me that they couldn't believe how good it was, and that they came back to eat it again because it was the best Amatriciana they had ever eaten; better than any in Lazio, Roma, or even Amatrice where the dish is a local specialty. "I kid you not." This was of the one of the greatest compliments that I've ever received in my professional culinary career, "Truly."

AMATRICIANA SAUCE
alla BELLINO

3 medium onions, sliced thinly. ¼ cup olive oil
1 teaspoon crushed red pepper, 1 Tbs. minced
fresh Rosemary
1 lb. smoked bacon and ½ lb. pancetta diced
2-28 oz. cans crushed tomatoes
3 cloves garlic, minced
kosher or sea salt and black pepper to taste
1 & 1/2 lbs. imported Italian Bucatini or
other pasta

1. Place bacon and pancetta in a large frying pan and cook over very low heat to render fat (about 12 minutes). Do not brown or let bacon get hard or crispy.

2. Remove bacon and pancetta from pan and set aside. Drain all but 3 tablespoons of fat from pan. Add olive oil and onions to pan and sauté over low heat for about 12 minutes. Add garlic and red pepper, sauté for three minutes.

3. Add tomatoes, bacon, and pancetta. Simmer for 30 minutes.

4. Add rosemary. Simmer for 15 minutes.

5. Cook Bucatini or other pasta. Drain pasta, sprinkle with olive oil. Add sauce, mix and plate. Serve with grated Parmigiano.

RAGU BOLOGNESE

"There is no greater culinary taste than the marriage of fresh pasta and a properly made Ragu Bolognese"

Marcella Hazan

RECIPE:

2 tablespoons olive oil
1 medium onion, minced
2 celery stalks & I carrot minced
2 lbs. ground beef and 1 lb. ground veal
2 1/2 cups Red Wine
1 cup chicken broth
2-28 ounce cans crushed San Marzano Tomatoes
1 oz. dried Porcini Mushrooms, soak in hot water
10 minutes to soften Mushrooms
5 tablespoons of sweet butter

Preparation:

1. Put olive oil, celery, onion, and minced carrot in a large pot. Sauté over a low flame for 5 minutes. Add ground meats to pot and cook until the meat has lost its raw color. Do not brown the meat or it will get hard. Break the meat up with a wooden spoon as you are cooking it.

2. Drain the fat off the meat mixture in a strainer. Put the drained meat back in the pot and season with Salt and Pepper.

3. Add wine and cook over high heat until the wine is reduced by half. Add tomatoes, Porcini and broth.

4. Cook the sauce over the lowest flame possible for 2 ½ hours while stirring every few minutes to keep the sauce from burning.

5. When sauce is finished cooking, turn off flame and stir butter into sauce.

6. Cook the pasta of your choice, Tagiatelle (Fettuccine) is most traditional for Bolognese Sauce, but you may use Spaghetti, Rigatoni, Fusilli, or any pasta you like.

7. Drain the cooked pasta and mix it with some of the sauce and a knob of butter. Serve with grated Parmigiano.

RIGATONI al FORNO

This is a great dish for parties and large groups of people. It is delicious and it can be made hours ahead of time or the day before a party and reheated in the oven when ready to serve. Also, if you prefer Ziti or some other short maccheroni to rigatoni, of course you can use any number of short pasta. I like rigatoni the best, but if you like Ziti and use Ziti in this recipe, then it would be an awesome "Soup-ed Up" version of Baked Ziti. Go for it, it's Abondanza!

1 lb. mozzarella cut into ½ inch cubes
1 cup ricotta
2 lbs. rigatoni, 1 ½ grated Parmigiano
1 lbs. sweet sausage simmered in water
for 12 minutes
Meatballs from Meatball recipe rolled into
1" diameter each
8 cups tomato sauce from previous recipe

1. Prepare Tomato Sauce and Meatballs from previous recipes. Roll the meatballs into 1" Meatballs. Roast the Meatballs in 350 degree oven for 15 minutes.

2. Cook the rigatoni for a few minutes less than Package states (about 7 minutes) as it will cook further in oven.

3. In a large baking pan that will be big enough to hold the ingredients, line the bottom of pan with tomato sauce.

4. Mix the cooked pasta with 5 cups of sauce, Mozzarella and slice Sausage.

5. Place half the mixture into pan. Put a light coat of sauce over the mixture. Dot with ½ the meatballs and Ricotta and sprinkle with some Parmigiano. Repeat this procedure until the pan is full.

6. Bake for 50 minutes at 350 degrees.

7. Plate and serve with grated Pecorino or Parmigiano Reggiano Cheese.

MUSSELS MARINARA

I remember a time back in the 60's when practically no one in America ate Mussels except we Italians. They were one of my mother's favorites and she would often send me to Bella Pizza on Park Avenue to get her an order. She loved them, Lucia Bellino, and I learned from a very young age to love them too.

Mussels Marinara are oh-so-tasty. The mussels, the marinara, and dipping the crusty Italian Bread into the garlic laden, mussel flavored sauce, is one of life's great treats, and not to mention, quite healthy as well, the mussels, tomato, garlic, and olive oil, all being quite good for you.

The place they eat more mussels than anywhere else in Italy is in the beautiful city by the bay, Napoli, or Naples to most. Yes, Neapolitans love them, and they are quite abundant in and around The Bay of Naples and all along The Amalfi Coast. God, what could be better, Mussels, Napoli, The Amalfi Coast? Not much I tell you. I will never forget a particular incident involving mussels. It was on my third trip to Italy and the lovely city of Naples, way back in 1987. I was walking around the city when I found myself at the Castelo dell Uvo (The Egg Castel). The Castel dell Ovo is on an island. The current Castel which is a fortress is on the island of Megeride. The Castel was built in the 1500's, but the island has had previous Castel/Fortress since Roman Times where the last Roman Emperor

Romulus Augustolus was exiled. Anyway, for the past 100 years the island has become a small fishing village and has for the past 50 years a marina and area with a some wonderful Seafood Restaurants and a place where young Italian couples go to take wedding pictures.

So, I was walking around the Castel Ovo one day and as I was walking by the back of one of these seafood specialty restaurants there was an old man behind the restaurant sitting at a wooden table cleaning mussels. He saw me and started talking to me and asked me where I was from. "New York, " I said. He told me his name was Giovanni and that he spoke such good English because he worked for years as a cook at a Diamond Mine in South Africa. He told me that this restaurant called Trattoria Cozze specialized in Mussels (Cozze in Italian). It sounded great to me, so I took a picture of the affable Giovanni and told him that I would return for dinner. I did. I will never forget that dinner. It was wonderful. I sat at a table outside, right by the water and will never forget when a cook pulled a plastic crate that was filled with live fresh mussels from the water (the Bay of Naples) right next to my table. I ordered two mussel based dishes, Caponata Napolitana and Spaghetti con Cozze. Now this Caponata is not the famous Sicilian Eggplant dish you might or might-not be thinking of. It was called Caponata, but over there in Napoli it is a salad made with greens served over a crisp Italian bread biscuit with wedges of juicy ripe tomatoes, big Green Olives, and Mussels of course. It was marvelous. I have never seen this before or after, but loved it, and have recreated it myself a number of times at a few of my dinner parties. After the tasty Caponata (Neapolitan Mussel Salad) I had my Spaghetti with Mussels (Spaghetti can Cozze), which was excellent as well. I had a glass of nice local Greco di Tufo, but no dessert. Dessert and coffee I would have later at a caffe in the Galleria.

A couple weeks later when I was showing my pictures at work, a guy Gino I worked with who was from Napoli flipped out as I sorted through the pictures. "Oh my God, that's my uncle Giovanni," he said as I came to the picture of Giovanni cleaning mussels at the restaurant. Pretty funny, and it's moments and memories like these that make life so interesting some times. "Mussels in Napoli, New York or wherever you may be."

MUSSELS MARINARA

INGREDIENTS:

2 lbs. Prince Edward Island Mussels, cleaned
4 cloves of Garlic, peeled and sliced thin
6 tablespoons Olive Oil
Pinch of Pepperoncino (Red Pepper Flakes)
¼ cup White Wine
1 ½ cup water
3 cups Tomato Sauce
¼ Fresh Chopped Italian Parsley

1. In a small pan, Sauté Garlic in Olive Oil over med-ium heat for 4 minutes. Add red pepper flakes and cook 30 seconds more.

2. Put white wine in a pot large enough to hold all of the Mussels. Turn on heat to high, and cook until wine is reduced by half, about 5 minutes. Add mussels and water and cover. Cook over high heat until all the mussels open. You will have to stir with a large spoon to or 3 times to move the mussels around. Keep the pot covered so the mussels will steam. When just about all the mussels have opened, turn off heat. Discard any mussels that have not opened.

3. When the mussels are cooking, add tomato sauce to pan with garlic and olive oil. Turn heat on to medium and cook about 6 minutes.

4. Once the mussels are all cooked and you have discarded any mussels that did not open, remove Mussels from pot and place in a large serving bowl or individual serving bowls.

5. Pour mussel cooking liquid in pan with Marinara Sauce, heat over medium heat while stirring for five minutes.

6. Pour Sauce over Mussels and serve with toasted Italian Bread.

SHRIMP SCAMPI

Shrimp Scampi. Now that's Italian, Italian American that is, and one of Italian-America's most craved dishes at that. It's tasty as Hell. You gotta love it! Shrimp Scampi is an Italian-American Classic. It is one of those great Italian-American Standards that was hugely popular in the 60's, 70's, and 80's, but waned when Italian-American so called Red-Sauce-Joints started to be looked-down-upon in stature and seriousness. Old-Timers still love the dish and ask for it to this very day.

Scampi is actually the Italian word for a small half Shrimp half Lobster looking crustacean found in and around the Mediterranean. It looks just like a shrimp with claws. So Shrimp Scampi actually translates to "Shrimp Shrimp" and is half Italian (Scampi) and half English in name. Shrimp in English meaning Shrimp and Scampi the Italian word for a shrimp-like crustacean. Wow, now that's a whole lot of Shrimp.

These days, there has been a great revival of the tasty old-school Italian Red Sauce Dishes. Meatballs are now hugely popular, with Chicken and Veal Parm following right behind. I've seen a bit of a revival of our old pal *Shrimp Sca*mpi but not to a huge extent. Old-Timers you've always loved it, and for all you younger people out there if you've never had it, it's high time you did, "You're sure to love it."

SHRIMP SCAMPI
"It's Shrimp Shrimp"

INGREDIENTS:

2 lbs. large Shrimp, peeled and deveined
5 tablespoons Olive Oil
4 tablespoons Butter
4 cloves Garlic, peeled and sliced thin
Sea Salt and Black Pepper
¼ cup dry White Wine
Juice from 1 Lemon
¼ Chopped Italian Parsley

1. Heat a large frying pan on medium heat. Add Olive Oil and half the butter. Add Garlic and cook until garlic just starts to show a slight brown color. Turn the heat to high and add Shrimp. Cook until all the shrimp lose their raw color.

2. Remove the Shrimp to warm plate and keep on the side. Add wine and turn heat up high. Cook until wine is reduced by half.

3. Add lemon juice and cook 30 seconds. Add remaining butter. Turn heat to high and cook for 30 seconds. Add shrimp and cook over high heat for 1 minute.

4. Turn off heat, add Parsley and stir. Serve Shrimp Scampi on its own, with steamed spinach, Rice Pilaf, or whatever you like. Enjoy!

SHRIMP Fra DIAVOLO

Shrimp Fra Diavolo is a much-favored dish among the Italian-American community in America. The dish is an Italian-American invention and not to be found in Italy as is the case with its slightly more elegant and expensive brother Lobster Fra Diavolo. Fra Diavolo translates from Italian to Brother (Fra), Devil (Diavolo). This dish is mostly consumed in restaurants as a special treat, but some like to make it at home as well as naturally it will considerably cut the cost, as you could probably feed two or three people Shrimp or Lobster Fra Diavolo for the price it would cost you at a restaurant for just one person. A great idea, which I have never seen anyone else do, but I came up with is to make a combination of Lobster & Shrimp fra Diavolo, making the dish with half Lobster and half Shrimp. Most often Shrimp and Lobster Fra Diavolo is served over a bed of Linguine or Spaghetti but if you'd like to cut down on carbs, steamed or sautéed spinach or any other vegetable can be served with the Fra Diavolo as well.

DUE DIAVOLAO
SHRIMP & LOBSTER Fra DIAVOLO

Ingredients:

1 ½ pounds Shrimp, peeled and deveined (or Lobster)
4 tablespoons Olive Oil, Sea Salt & Black Pepper
1 to 2 tablespoons Pepperoncino (Red Pepper Flakes)
1 tablespoon dry Oregano
1 small onion, peeled and diced fine
1 – 28 ounce can whole Plum Tomatoes
2 tablespoons fresh chopped Flat Leaf Parsley
¼ cup water

1. Crush tomatoes, making them broken but in small chunks. Keep on the side.

2. Place olive oil and onions in a large frying pan that is large enough to hold tomatoes and shrimp or Lobster. Cook onions on low heat for 5 minutes. Add garlic and cook on low heat for 4 minutes.

3. Turn heat up and cook to garlic just looks to be turning a little brown. Add Red Pepper and cook one minute longer. Add Oregano and tomatoes.

4. Add water and turn heat to high until tomatoes start bubbly. Turn heat down to medium and cook for 15 minutes.

5. Add Shrimp and cook on medium heat until the Shrimp lose their raw color, about 4 - 5 minutes. If using Lobster, boil lobsters in shell, let cool. Remove Lobster Meat from shell and heat in Fra Diavolo Sauce on low heat for 4 minutes.

6. Serve the Fra Diavolo over a bed of Spaghetti, Linguine, steamed or Sautéed Spinach or Whatever vegetable you like.

NOTE: You can make this dish as hot as you like or less hot by varying the amount of Pepperoncino (Hot Red Pepper Flakes).

CHICKEN CUTLETS

Chicken Cutlets are quite popular among Italian Americans. They are tasty and quite versatile as you can make any number of dishes from this base of breaded fried chicken cutlets, or simply eat them on there owned once breaded and fried with a Mixed or Arugala Salad over the top or on the side, you have a much cheaper and equally tasty version of the famed, but pricey Veal Milanese. Use *Chicken Cutlets* to make *Pollo Milanese*. Once you have breaded fried chicken cutlets you can make *Pollo alla Sorrentino* by baking the cutlets with tomato sauce, fried Eggplant and Mozzarella on top. These chicken cutlets are the base of *Chicken Parmigiano* which you make by placing in a baking pan with Tomato Sauce, Parmigiano, and Mozzarella baked on top of the fried chicken cutlets. It's as simple as that. And don't forget you can make Chicken Parm Sandwiches too.

CHICKEN PARMIGIANO

Chicken Parmigiano, along with it's veal counter-part of Veal Parmigiano is Italian-American to the core. Created by Italian Americans in America, it is a dish greatly loved by not only Italian-Americans, but by millions of Americans of every ethnic background imaginable. It is a dish that is hugely popular, and along with Spaghetti & Meatballs, and Veal Parmigiano, 100s of *Millions* of dishes of each have been served over the years.

Chicken Parmigiano, or as many know it Chicken Parmesan, or Chicken Parm is mostly sold in rest-aurants. It's a wonder the dish isn't made at home more often. It's quite easy to make, especially if you already have some tomato sauce on hand, which is required in making the dish. And once you know how to make Chicken Parmigiano, which again is pretty simple, you will also then be able to make *Veal Parmigiano*, which is made exactly the same way, just substituting Veal for the Chicken.

I myself prefer Chicken Parmigiano to Veal Parm, and it's cheaper to boot. One alternative if you are thinking about having Veal Parmigiano but don't want to pay the high price for the Veal is to make it with pork cutlets. The pork is much cheaper than the veal, and to me it's just as tasty.

Note: To make the chicken cutlets, use first 6 ingredients from following Chicken Parm recipe, and follow steps 1, 3, and 4 and you've got nice tasty Chicken Cutlets alla Italiano. Buon Appetito!

CHICKEN PARMIGIANO RECIPE:

4 Boneless Chicken Breast (pounded thin)
Salt & Black Pepper
1 cup flour
1 cup unseasoned breadcrumbs
2 Large Eggs (beaten)
2 cups Tomato Sauce
½ cup grated Parmigiano or Grana Padano Cheese
½ pound Mozzarella Cheese, sliced thin
½ cup Canola, Peanut, or Vegetable Oil for frying

1. Place the Breadcrumbs, Eggs, and Flour, all in their own separate bowls. Season each with a little Salt & Pepper.

2. In a small pot, heat the tomato sauce.

3. One by one, dredge each Chicken Breast into the flour. Shake off excess flour, then dip into the beaten Eggs. Then place the chicken into the breadcrumbs, pressing crumbs into the chicken, covering the entire surface of each Chicken Breast.

4. Heat oil in frying pan so it is hot enough that it will immediately start frying the chicken when it's put into the pan, cook all the chicken about 3 minutes on each side, then remove from pan.

5. Place the chicken breast in a shallow pan. Turn oven on to 400 degrees. Coat the top of each Chicken Breast with tomato sauce. Sprinkle grated Cheese over the chicken and evenly top with the Mozzarella Cheese. Bake for 8 minutes at 400 degrees.

VEAL PARM Too!"

Here's how! So as we have already mentioned, that if you know how to make Chicken Parm, then you know how to make Veal Parm, just substitute veal scallopini or veal cutlets for the chicken and you make the Veal Parmigiano exactly the same way as the Chicken Parm. Also, *pork* is another great choice. Tell your butcher what you need and get him to cut you nice pork scallopinini's or cutlets, and substitute the *pork* for the chicken and follow the same procedure, and Voila, you've got Pork Parm.

PS ... Just a little interesting fact about Veal Parm and Veal Milanese. Veal Parmigiano is a very popular dish in the heavily Italian populated country of Argentina. Even more famous in Argentina besides its very famous Steaks and mixed meat grill platters, is the fact that they love Veal Milanese, a true Italian classic from Italy. And guess what? The Argentines eat more plates of Veal Milanese than they do in Italy or anywhere else in the World. And if you're ever in Argentina and are in the mood for a Veal Parm, the name is different there, where it is known as Veal Napolitana. Basta!

Yes, It's Italian!
Italian-American!"

DBZ

CHICKEN VESUVIO alla SINATRA

The dish Chicken alla Vesuvio named for the famous Volcano near Naples, Italy is a big favorite in the great city of Chicago. You won't find this dish in Italy as it was created by an Italian-American Chef in the great city of Chicago, and believed to be first created at Vesuvio Restaurant on Wacker Drive in the 1930's. The dish was a favorite of Frank Sinatra and a recipe in the style that Frank liked it, can be found (no Garlic) below. Cook it up, put on a Sinatra disc and enjoy.

INGREDIENTS:

1 - 3 1/2-pound chicken, cut into 8 pieces
¼ cup Olive Oil
3 Idaho Potatoes, cut in half, then into 10 pieces
1 Red Bell Pepper cut into 1" thick strips
1 medium Yellow Onion
1 small Red Onion
1 teaspoon crushed Red Pepper flakes
Salt and pepper to taste
1 -10 package Frozen Peas

1. Preheat the oven to 425 degrees. Season the chicken with Salt and Pepper.

2. Put potatoes in a pot of boiling water and let boil for 4 minutes. Drain potatoes and set aside.

3. Sauté chicken in a large frying pan with half the olive oil over medium heat for about 12-15 minutes, until all of the chicken is nicely browned. This is the most important step of the dish, you want to get the chicken nice and brown. Add half Red Pepper Flakes and cook for 2 minutes.

4. Transfer the chicken to a baking pan.

5. Add remaining olive oil to frying pan that chicken was browned in. Add onions and Red Bell Pepper, season with salt & pepper.
6. Cook Bell Peppers and onions over medium heat with remaining red pepper flakes for 8 minutes. Add potatoes and cook over high heat for 5 minutes.

7. Add potatoes, onions, and bell peppers to pan with chicken and mix.

8. Cook in a 375 degree oven for about 25 minutes, until chicken is fully cooked. Add Peas to pan and cook another 6 minutes at 400 degrees.

9. Serve chicken and vegetables with a Green Salad or sautéed green vegetables on the side.

Note: Believe it or not, Frank Sinatra wasn't big on garlic. Most recipes for Chicken Vesuvio contain garlic which we like, but this recipe for Chicken Vesuvio alla Sinatra does not. If you want garlic, you can add 3 to 6 cloves at step 6. Some add wine, we think it's better without it, so did Frank.

Veal Sorrentino
and "Chicken too!"

Veal Sorrentino is another favorite of the Italian-American table. Not as popular with the rest of America as Chicken Parmigiano and Veal Parmigiano are, but Veal and or Chicken Sorrentino are more of an Italian-American thing. OK, if you now know how to make Chicken Parmigiano, as per the preceding recipe, you can easily make Veal and or Chicken Sorrentino. The ingredients and preparation are the same, with the addition of a slice of fried eggplant and thin sliced Prosciutto in-between the tomato sauce on top of the chicken breast and the Mozzarella.

To make Chicken Sorrentino, you will use the same proceeding recipe with all the same ingredients, and the addition of four thin slices of Prosciutto and eggplant. To make the eggplant, cut four thin slices from a long eggplant, in lengthwise slices. Season the eggplant with salt and pepper, and dredge in flour, shaking off any excess flour. Fry the eggplant in the same oil as you fry the chicken. Fry the eggplant for about 3 minutes until golden brown, turning once, and then drain.

To assemble the Chicken (or Veal) Sorrentino, place the cooked fried chicken cutlets in a shallow baking pan. Coat each with tomato sauce. Then top with one slice each of fried eggplant. Lay a slice of Prosciutto over the eggplant, sprinkle with grated

Parmigiano, Pecorino, or Grana Padano Cheese. Top with slices of Mozzarella and bake in a 400 degree oven for about 12 minutes, until the Mozzarella has melted.

This dish is best served with a nice sautéed green vegetable like; Escarole, Spinach, or Broccoli Rabe (Rapini). Many like, pasta on the side. I'd rather have this dish with a green veg, but if you want a side of pasta with it, go right ahead. That's Italian, Italian-American!

Note: This dish can be made as above with Prosciutto, which we love, but if you prefer not to, many make it without the Prosciutto, it's OK. Also you can make the dish without any flour at all, simply by cooking both the eggplant and the chicken in a pan with olive oil without any flour or breadcrumbs. Note that the dish is made with the flour and breadcrumbs by most, as this is in the standard recipe. We realize some have gluten allergies so it is perfectly fine to make it without flour if you diet calls for it.

VEAL MILANESE

Veal Milanese? Now that's Italian! Italian from Italy that is, and totally authentic to Italy and not an Italian-American invention. Veal Milanese is particularly loved by New York and New Jersey Italian-Americans, but it's a dish that is not often eaten at home. It is most often eaten in Italian Restaurants. Veal Milanese is a dish that when made in its most classic form and of the original recipe is made with a rib veal-chop that is pounded thin, then breaded, then fried in a combination of butter and oil to browned, crisp, and crunchy. It is put on a plate and topped with a salad of Arugala & Tomato. It is simple and delicious. Veal Milanese is simple and delicious, but cheap it's not. This dish can cost you anywhere from about $29 to $42 a pop, with the average being about $39 in a restaurant. Not cheap! You can make it at home for about $10 or $12, considerably cheaper than 39 dollars. But guess what? Just like with our friend Veal Parmigiano, Veal Milanese can be made with chicken or pork. Yes, it's no longer Veal Milanese, but Pork or Chicken Milanese. But guess what? It taste just as good, and it's way cheaper. So if, you have a hankering for some Veal Milanese, but don't want to spend $39 plus tip, plus tax, and you've got to have a least one glass of wine in a restaurant, that Veal Milanese with all the rest is gonna cost you about $65 or so. Dam! But you've got alternatives. You can make Veal Milanese at home for $10 to $12, or you can make Pork or Chicken Milanese for $3 or $4 a serving. Not a bad alternative.

Oh, and by the way, did you know that Veal Milanese was one of Frank Sinatra's favorite dishes? Yes, ol Blue Eyes loved it, along with; a simple bowl of Spaghetti Pomodoro (Tomato Sauce), Clams Posillipo, Sausages, Meatballs, and of course Sunday Sauce. As many know, Patsy's on West 56th Street in New York was Sinatra's all-time favorite restaurant. He loved and adored the place, and ate there for more than 50 years. Frank liked his Veal Milanese at Patsy's and he liked it a certain way, extra thin and extra crisp. Veal Milanese is already pounded thin to begin with, but Frank liked his even thinner, and at Patsy's they always granted Frank's request and gave him what he wanted, which was good-old, no-fuss Italian Food prepared to perfection. Basta!

VEAL MILANESE "The RECIPE"

INGREDIENTS:

4 Veal Cutlets from your butcher, or pork or chicken
1-1/2 cups plain breadcrumbs
1 ½ cups flour
3 eggs, Salt & Black Pepper
4 cups Arugala, 1 cup cherry tomatoes cut in half
2 lemons cut in half
Vegetable Oil for frying and half stick of butter
2 lemons cut in half
6 tablespoons Olive Oil, Salt & Pepper to Taste
2 tablespoons Red Wine Vinegar

Preparation:

1. Place four, eggs, and bread crumbs each in their own separate bowls.

2. Season cutlets with Salt & Pepper. Season eggs, Flour and breadcrumbs with salt & pepper

3. Dredge each veal cutlet in flour, and shake off excess flour.

4. Then dredge veal in eggs, shaking off excess flour before putting in to breadcrumbs.

5. Completely coat veal cutlets with breadcrumbs. Press bread crumbs in to the cutlets. Set Aside.

6. Heat oil over medium heat in a frying pan that is big enough to cook 2 cutlets at a time.

7. When oil is hot enough for frying, add butter and turn heat to high. Add 2 of the breaded cutlets and fry on each side to slightly golden brown. Remove fried cutlets to a plate with paper towels and keep warm.

8. Fry other 2 cutlets until golden brown on each side.

9. Place Arugala and Tomatoes in a mixing bowl. Olive Oil and Vinegar. Season with Salt & Pepper to taste. Toss Salad.

10. Place each cooked Veal Cutlet on a plate each. top each cutlet with salad. Place a half lemon on each plate and serve your Veal Milanese

VEAL PICCATA

Ingredients:

12 Veal Scallopini from your butcher
3 tablespoons vegetable oil
1 cup flour in a shallow bowl
Salt & Black Pepper
2 tablespoons of Butter cut into 6 pieces
3 Lemons
2 tablespoon Fresh Parsley, chopped fine

1. Cut 12 thin slices from 1 ½ lemons. Squeeze remaining 1 ½ lemons of their juice and set aside.

2. Heat a frying pan that is large enough to hold half of your veal, 6 pieces. Add vegetable oil.

3. Season Veal Scaloppini's with Salt & Pepper and all in flour. Shake off excess flour.

4. Place half the veal in the pan with hot oil and cook for about 1 ½ on each side.

5. Finish cooking all the veal and leave in a plate on the side, keeping warm.

6. When all the veal has cooked, drain oil out of pan. Return pan to stove and set over a high flame. Add lemon juice and cook while scraping the bottom of pan to remove brown bits on bottom of pan. This is called de-glazing, and there is a lot of flavor in those brown bits, which get incorporated into the sauce, helping to make it so tasty. Cook 1 minute.

7. Turn off heat. Add butter to pan. Swirl the pan in a circular motion which will help combine the butter with lemon and pan juices into the Piccata Sauce.

8. Return all Veal to pan and turn heat on a low flame. Cook for 1 minute over low heat while swirling pan in a circular motion. Turn heat off.

9. Place 3 pieces of veal on each of 4 plates. Pour equal amounts of sauce on each plate over the Veal. Sprinkle chopped Parsley over each dish. Place a thin slice of lemon on each piece of Veal and serve.

Serves 4

NOTE: Serve the Veal Piccata with roast or boiled Potatoes, Sautéed Spinach, or Boiled Carrots.

Uncle Tony's Veal Marsala

This isn't your usual Veal Marsala, but quite frankly the best. Best for me anyway. Most Veal Marsala dishes are made with Veal Scallopini sautéed with mushrooms and Marsala Wine from Sicily. Uncle Tony's Veal Marsala uses veal shoulder and is braised instead of sautéed, making the dish much more versatile and great to cook for larger groups of people.

My Uncle Tony grew up on Main Street in Lodi, New Jersey in the 1930's above my Grandfathers Shoemaker Shop with my Mom, her sister my Aunt Lily, and my Uncles Frank and James, as well. Yes, my grandfather from Lercara Friddi, Sicily (same town as Sinatra & Lucky Luciano) had a shoemaker shop on Main Street in Lodi, New Jersey, a town that was at the time 100% Italian, so Uncle Frank told me so one day. Next door to my grandfather Phillipo's shoemaker shop was the Scarlotta Meat Market. One of the sons of the owner, Jimmy Scarlotta, was my Uncle Tony's childhood best friend. My Uncle Tony used to hang out at the meat market quite a lot and even worked there for a couple years. So my uncle Tony knows his way around meat, and he's very particular about it.

Uncle Tony's Marsala is the best I've ever had, and it's a great dish for a party as you can make it ahead unlike the usual Veal Marsala which is made alla minute, and has to be eaten immediately. Uncle Tony's Marsala can be made ahead of time, held and served whenever you're ready, "e' Molto Buona."

Uncle Tony's Veal Marsala
"The Recipe"

1 ½ pounds Veal Shoulder, cut in 2" square pieces
1 small onion, peeled and diced fine
6 ounces Button Mushrooms
2 ounces Dry Porcini Mushrooms, reconstituted
½ cup good quality Sweet Marsala Wine
1 tablespoon Butter, 2 tablespoons Olive Oil
1 tablespoon flour
¼ cup chopped fresh Italian Parsley (not dried)

1. Heat a large frying pan that is large enough to hold all the veal. Add olive oil.

2. Pat all the veal dry with a paper towel. Season the veal with salt & Black Pepper. Add veal to pan. Brown over high heat until all the veal is nicely browned.

3. Add ¾ of the Marsala Wine and let reduce to half its original volume. Once you add the wine, scrape the bottom of pan with a wooden spoon. This loosens the brown bits that stick to bottom of the pan. These brown bits are full of flavor and are key in making a good sauce.

4. Once the Marsala has reduced by half, remove the Veal and the cooking juice from pan and set aside.

5. Add 2 tablespoons olive oil and 1 of butter to Pan. Add fresh mushrooms and cook over Medium heat until mushrooms are cooked through. About 6-7 minutes. Remove from Pan and set aside.

6. Add 2 tablespoons of butter to pan. Add veal back to pan without juices. Turn heat on low and cook for 1 minute. Sprinkle flour evenly over veal while stirring. Cook at low heat for 2 minutes. Add remaining Marsala Wine and Cook at low heat 2 minutes.

7. Add veal juices to pan. Add Porcini Mushrooms. Add 1 cup chicken stock. Simmer Veal for 1 hour and 15 minutes over very low heat.
8. Add fresh mushrooms to pan, cook for 15 minutes more. Veal should be nice and tender. Serve Veal Marsala with boiled or mashed Potatoes. Serve each person and sprinkle fresh chopped Parsley over top. Enjoy

Chicken Cacciatore

When I was a kid Chicken Cacciatore was a pretty popular dish. Not so much any more, but old timers still love it, and newcomers should get into it as well. This was one of my mother's favorites and she used to make it all the time. We loved it, and so will you.

Ingredients:

1 whole broiler chicken cut into 10 pieces, 2 wings, 2 thighs, 2 legs, and 2 Breast cut in 4 pieces
1 medium onion, peeled and diced
6 cloves of Garlic, peeled and sliced
1 Red Bell Pepper, cleaned and cut in to 1 ½" strips
1 can of Whole San Marzano Tomatoes
¼ teaspoon Red Pepper Flakes
Sea Salt & Black Pepper

1. Season chicken with salt & pepper. Cook chicken in a large frying pan over high heat until all of the chicken is nicely browned. About 12 minutes.

2. Add Bell Pepper, and cook on low flame for 8 minutes on a low flame. Add onions, cook for 5 minutes. Add garlic, cook for 2 minutes.

3. Turn heat to high, add tomatoes. Cook for 2 minutes at high heat. Season with Salt & Black Pepper. Lower heat to low, and simmer for 20 minutes. Serve with boiled potatoes or whatever vegetable you like.

Note: When browning the chicken, it is very important to get the chicken nice and brown. In browning the chicken as in any dish where you are browning poultry, or meat, the browning is caramelizing the meat and brings an abundance of flavor to it, as well as properly seasoning with salt & pepper, so make sure you do a good job and get the chicken nice and brown before it cooks with the tomatoes, onion, and peppers. Once the chicken goes in with the remaining ingredients it will no longer be able to brown.

SHOEMAKERS CHICKEN
"Pollo al' Scarpariello"

    Chicken Scarpariello, "ShoeMakers Chicken. "That's what my Grandfather Phillipo was, a shoemaker from Lercara Friddi, Sicily. The same town that Frank Sinatra's grandfather was also a Shoemaker in. My Mother's Father Phillipo Bellino and Mother (Josephina) immigrated to the United States through the Port of New York at Ellis Island in 1904. My Grandfather Phillipo Bellino opened a shoemaker shop on Main St., in Lodi, New Jersey (Soprano Territory). This dish is not that well known by most Americans apart from those of Italian Ancestry, of which this dish is a great favorite.

SHOEMAKER'S CHICKEN

Ingredients:

1 whole broiler chicken cut up into 8 pieces
4-6 links of fresh Italian pork sausage, either sweet or hot, or a combination
2 sprigs of rosemary
2 red bell peppers cut into ¾ inch slices
8 garlic cloves
crushed Red Pepper
Salt & Black Pepper to taste

Preparation:

1. Blanche sausage in simmering water for six minutes.

2. Season chicken with salt and pepper. Place chicken in a large frying pan with olive oil and brown chicken on all sides for about 12 - 15 minutes until nicely browned and crisp. Lower heat to low and let chicken cook on low heat for 10-12 minutes. Turn chicken pieces once.

3. Remove chicken from pan to a platter. Cut sausage into four pieces each and brown in frying pan. Add peppers and cook with Sausage over medium heat for 7 minutes.

4. Add chicken back into pan. Cover pan and cook over a low flame for 5 minutes. Take cover off pan, add rosemary and continue cooking for 5 minutes.

5. Serve each person two to 3 pieces of chicken with sausages and peppers. Serve with a salad, roast or boiled potatoes, or any vegetable you like.

LEMON CHICKEN "RAO'S STYLE"

Rao's is the very famous East Harlem Italian Eatery that is filled with Celebrities, Wise Guys and Wannabe-Wise Guys, and guess what? You probably can't get in. Know why? Cause *Frankie No* says "No!" It's reserved for VIP, Celebs and those connected to Frankie, one Frank Pelligrino from Goodfellas and Soprano fame. You see, Frankie owns the place, and try if you will, it's the *hardest table in town* and it's all the way up in East Harlem, not downtown, Mid-Town or other prime-locals of Manhattan. If you ever get in, cherish the experience, if not, here's a recipe for their Famous Lemon Chicken. Make the Chicken, put on some Sinatra, Dino, Jerry Vale, and pretend. Pretend you're at Rao's of New York, a place you probably *"can't get in."*

INGREDIENTS:

1 cup fresh lemon juice
1 cup extra-virgin olive oil
1 tbsp. red wine vinegar
1 clove garlic, peeled and minced
1/2 tsp. dried oregano
Salt and freshly ground black pepper
1/4 cup chopped fresh parsley
1 Broiler Chicken, cut into 10 pieces; 2 wings, 2 legs,
2 thighs, and cut the 2 breast in half making 4 pieces

PREPARATION:

1. Season the chicken pieces with salt and black pepper.

2. Place all ingredients except the chicken, a quarter of the olive oil, and the parsley in a large glass or ceramic bowl. Set aside.

3. Turn oven on to 450 degrees.

4. Put a large frying pan that will be large enough to hole all the chicken on stove top. Turn heat on high. Add ¼ of the olive oil to frying pan. Heat 2 minutes, then add the chicken.

5. Brown chicken in frying pan for 12, turning the chicken pieces every 4 minutes or so until nicely browned. Place chicken in oven and cook for 15 minutes.

6. Add the lemon mixture to pan with chicken. Return to over and cook for 12 minutes.

7. Remove chicken from oven and peek into the inside of the chicken with a knife to make sure the chicken is cooked through and there is no blood. If there is blood, put chicken back in oven and let cook more until there is no more sign of blood on inside of chicken.

8. Place chicken on a place and keep warm in the oven turned down to 250 degree. Set frying pan with lemon juice mixture from chicken on top of the stove and cook over high heat for minutes. Remove from flame. Let cool down to warm for 5 minutes, then pour a little of the sauce over chicken and set the rest of the lemon sauce on the side. Sprinkle the fresh chopped Parsley over the chicken, serve and enjoy.

THE PORK STORE

The Pork Store, an Italian Pork Store is vital to the community, the Italian-American community. This is where you go to get your Sausages, Braciole, Pork Chops, Pasta, Olive Oil, vinegar, Parmigiano, Salami, Prosciutto, Olives, Anchovies, and all the things vital to living a normal & happy Italian-American life. If there is one? Just joking. Of course there is.

We previously mentioned going to a "good" Pork Store to get your fresh Italian Pork Sausages, Hot or Sweet. We needn't really mention the good in going to a Pork Store, as by definition a Pork Store is good. It's always good. I don't know why, they just always are. It's all the good food, must be. I've never ever seen or heard of a Pork Store not being good. They're great, as matter of fact! "Never" Bad. That's just the way it is. You can find good and bad restaurants, and though seldom a Pizzeria that's not good. Not so often. Yes there are many bad restaurants, Italian ones and otherwise, but I don't think you'll ever find a bad Pork Store, one that's not good. Never heard such a thing, doesn't exist.

Not much has ever been written on The Pork Store over the years. Don't know why, you could write a whole book on them. I was curious to see things written on the subject and there is practically nothing. However you will find a fair amount written on the subject in my book La Tavola, and here of course as well. Yes Pork Stores are great! Do you remember Satriale's Pork Store in The

Sopranos? My favorite Pork Store is just a couple blocks from my house, Faicco's where I can get all my kitchen needs; fresh Hot & Sweet Sausage of course, Olive Oil, homemade Sopressata, and Braciole, stuffed, tied and ready for cooking in gravy. And Faicco's like any good Pork Store makes the Best Sandwiches in the neighborhood. Try Capicola with Provolone. Yumm!

Did you know that there have been quite a number of unfortunate Italian-Americans over the years who have been displaced for one reason or another from cities and areas of great Italian-American enclaves like New York City, Philly, Jersey, Boston, Baltimore, New Orleans and such. People might have moved to places like Texas, Arizona, Iowa or wherever. Places where there were not many Italians, and worse yet, no good Italian Restaurants, Pastry Shops, Pizzerias, and Pork Stores. The great Italian-American writer Nick Pileggi in his book Wise Guy which was made into a the movie Goodfellas by Martin Scorsese where actor Ray Liotta playing true-life gangster Henry Hill portrays this "sad dilemma" quite well, when Henry is put into the Federal Witness Protection Program and relocated somewhere like Bumf_ck, Iowa where there are no good Pizza Parlors, Italian Restaurants, or Pork Stores in-sight. It's enough to make a grown man cry, and believe me, men have cried over not being able to obtain good fresh Italian-Sausages, Prosciutto, Parmigiano and other necessities to living a good, happy, healthy and contented life. Hope you have a good store near you.

PASTA FAZOOL
"Pasta Fagoli"

Pasta Fazool! That's what we Italian-Americans call it, Pasta & Bean Soup aka Pasta Fagoli! We need to give the Italian-American twist to our Italian Heritage of Pasta & Bean Soup, known in Italy as Pasta Fagoli. Hey, we're animated people, Italians. Some are livelier than others, especially in Brooklyn, the borough known by Brooklynite Italians as Brucilina. "Fug-get-about-it!"

As we love our Sunday Sauce, Sausage & Peppers, Meatball Parms, Espresso, and Cannoli, we're also quite fond of our Pasta Fazool, a long-time Italian-American favorite. There are a number of ways of making Pasta Fazool (Pasta Fagoli). The recipes may vary a little but basically they're pretty similar with slight variations here and there. Most use cannellini beans in making their version of Pasta Fagoli while others like to use red Borlotti Beans (Roman Beans). Some make theirs completely vegetarian, but most make it with a little pork product (not too much), like; Pancetta (Italian Un-Smoked Bacon), Guanciale (cured Pork Cheek), Prosciutto, or a Ham Hock. Some make their Pasta Fazool completely from scratch using dried beans while others use canned beans, which is perfectly fine, it's a lot easier and takes a whole lot less time, though if you want the most authentic Pasta Fazool, you'll make yours with the dried Cannellini or Borlotti Beans.

Pasta Fazool has been a staple of the Italian-American kitchen and households for more than 100 years now. As we know at the turn of The 19th Century (1900) American cities like New York, Boston, and Baltimore were filling up with a huge amount of Italian Immigrants, mostly from the South of Italy; Napoli, Sicily, Calabria, and Apulia. The vast majority of these immigrants were quite poor. They didn't have much money and had to let every dollar stretch as far as possible. To do this, they ate a lot of pasta, including Pasta Fazool, a soup utilizing a fair amount of pasta. Carry on the tradition and eat it too, and you don't have to call it Pasta Fagoli, it's "Pasta-Fazool."

HOW To MAKE PASTA FAZOOL

Ingredients:

2 medium onions, 3 celery stalks, 2 carrots, minced
½ lb. pancetta, minced finely. ¼ cup olive oil
8 cloves garlic, peeled and cut into thirds
1 lb. dried cannellini beans,
soaked in water overnight
2 sprigs fresh rosemary. 1 bay leaf
1 ½ cups canned plum tomatoes
4 cups chicken broth
4 cups water. Salt & pepper to taste
1 lb. Ditalini

Preparation:

1. Sauté pancetta in a large pot for 3 minutes. Add garlic & onions, and sauté for 6 minutes on low heat.

2. Add celery and carrots, and sauté for 4 minutes.

3. Add tomatoes, beans, broth, & water. Bring up to the boil, then lower to a slow simmer and cook for 1 ½ hours until the beans are tender.

4. Remove half the beans and mash through a food mill or puree in a blender.

5. Place the mashed beans back into the pot with the whole beans.

6. Put remainder of olive oil in a pan with 6 cloves of garlic, a bay leaf, and rosemary. Cook over medium heat for 6 minutes. This is called a perfume.

7. Strain the perfume into the pot of soup, mix and simmer the soup with perfume for 12 minutes.

8. Cook the ditalini according to instructions on.

9. To serve, put ½ cup cooked ditalini in a soup bowl. Fill the bowl with the bean soup. Sprinkle a little Extra-virgin olive oil over the soup. Pass around the grated Parmigiano and enjoy.

ITALIAN WEDDING SOUP
"Zuppa d'Mariata"

Italian Wedding Soup is one of the Soup-World's loveliest and most whimsical of soup, and it's the little Meatballs that do the trick. It's a wonder that this soup is not more popular in the U.S.. This tasty little soup has stayed mostly within the confines of the Italian-American conclave and has not gone into main-stream America in any big way. The soup Minestra d'Maritata as it is known in Italy, comes from the regions of Lazio (Rome) and the environs in and around Napoli (Naples) in Campania. The Minestra Maritata (Wedding Soup) became hugely popular in the Italian-American-Community where it is made in households all over the country. In the first half of the 20th Century Zuppa d'Mariata was served at many an Italian neighborhood wedding in New York, Philly, Providence, Pittsburgh, Chicago, and Jersey, in the days of weddings held in church basements, VFW Halls, at various Social Clubs, in someone's home or backyard. These were the days before $50,000 & $100,000 Weddings. Simple times, and I guarantee that most any home-made Italian Wedding Soup would taste better than 90% of anything you'd find at a catered wedding. The taste and variety of this soup just can't be beat. It's a whole meal in itself. You can make large Antipasto Platters to start, have the Wedding Soup for your main course with nice crusty Italian Bread and wine, and you're set with a complete meal. For dessert you'll have a homemade wedding cake, Cannoli's,

Italian Cookies, Coffee and Anisette. Basta, you're all set.

PS, Kids really love the little Meatballs in the Soup. "Kids of all ages that is!"

Recipe Italian Wedding Soup:

¾ lb. ground beef and ¾ lb. ground pork
½ cup grated Parmigiano, 1 clove garlic, minced
¼ fresh parsley, finely chopped. 1 bay leaf
1-3 lb. broiler chicken, 6 whole cloves garlic, peeled
8 cups water, 4 cups chicken broth
1 large onion, chopped. 2 carrots diced
1 head escarole, finely chopped

PREPARATION:

1. Combine ground meat, eggs, parsley, minced garlic, and Parmigiano. Season with salt & pepper. Shape into Meatballs, about the size of a large Marble. Set aside.

2. Place whole chicken, whole garlic, bay leaf, and water in a large pot and bring to the boil. Lower heat and simmer for 1 hour and 15 minutes.

3. Place meatballs in a lightly oiled baking pan and cook in a 350 Degree oven for 8 minutes.

4. Remove chicken from pot and set aside to cool. Add Carrots and onions to broth, cook for 12 minutes.

5. Blanche the Escarole for 5 minutes in boiling salted water. Drain the escarole and set aside.

6. Remove chicken meat from bones and dice. Add Meatballs and diced chicken meat to broth and simmer at the lowest flame for 7 minutes.

7. Add the escarole and simmer on low heat for 5 minutes. Turn off heat, and let the soup set for 5 minutes before serving.

8. Ladle soup into bowls, giving everyone at least 5 little meatballs. Pass the Parmigiano and Mangia Bene.

Note: You can substitute Sausage for the Meatballs, which is how some people make this soup. It's just as tasty and cuts down on some of the work. If doing so, substitute 1 ½ pounds of Italian Sweet Sausages for the meatballs. Lightly brown the links of sausage over low heat for 6 minutes. Remove from pan and cut each link into 6 equal size pieces, then add to soup in the same point (step 6) and cook over low heat in soup for 12 minutes.

FAMOUS ITALIAN-AMERICANS
"Just for Fun"

Frank Sinatra …. The Greatest Entertainer Ever
Dean Martin (Dino Paul Crocetti)
aka "Dino Martini"
Joe DiMaggio a.ka. "Joltin Joe DiMaggio"
Al Pacino …. One of America's Greatest Actors
Robert DeNiro … One of The Greatest Actors Ever
Frankie Valli … Lead Singer of The Four Seasons
Vince Lombardi .. Great NFL Football Coach
Mario Cuomo … Governor of New York
Madonna (Madonna Louis Ciccione) … Singer
Tony Bennett (Anthony Dominick Benedetto)
Leonardo DiCaprio … Famous American Actor
Annette Funicello … Mouseketeer, Singer, Actress
Frankie Avalon (Francis Thomas Avallone)
Connie Francis … Singer, Actress
Perry Como (Pierino Ronald Como) .. Singer
Jerry Vale (Luigi Vitaliano) … Singer
Bobby Darren (Walden Robert Cassotto) Singer, Actor
Bobby Rydell (Robert Louis Ridarelli)
Fiorello LaGuardia … Mayor of New York City
Frank Zappa … Rock Musician
Francis Ford Coppola Movie Director, Vineyard Owner
Martin Scorsese … Movie Director
Joe Pesci … Actor
Mario Batali … Famous Chef
Joe Pepitone Professional-Baseball Player
Salvatore "Lucky Luciano" Famed Mafia Boss
Nicholas Pileggi … Writer

LENTIL SOUP
"Zuppa di Lenticchie"

Lentil Soup is quite amazing. It's inexpensive, highly nutritious, and extremely versatile. You can eat it just about any time of day; for Breakfast, Lunch, Dinner or anytime in-between. Me? I just love it! It's my favorite soup and I make it all the time. Make a big batch and you'll get numerous meals out of it. This recipe serves about 16. From this base soup, I eat it different ways at times. Sometimes I'll cook up some small maccheroni, coat it with olive oil and butter and use a bit of the lentil soup as a sauce, sprinkling on grated cheese of course. Some times I'll throw in a hard-boiled egg that is cut in four, or I'll throw in a bunch of frozen peas to the base soup.

These things you do after this soup has already been cooked and you're heating up a bowl for quick tasty meal, it gives you variety. One thing you can do when you are making the soup from scratch, or even at a later time after the soup has been made, is put in some Sweet Italian Sausages. Yumm, that's one great Italian meal, Zuppa di Lentiche con Salsice. I guarantee it just can't be beat. Try it some time; and I think you'll agree.

LENTIL SOUP Recipe:

10 oz. dry lentils, 4 tablespoons olive oil
3 medium onions, diced. 3 cloves garlic, chopped
3 stalks celery, chopped. 3 carrots, diced large
1-1/2 cups plum tomatoes chopped
½ cup diced Ham, Bacon, or Pancetta
2 cups chicken broth
6 cups water
Salt & Black Pepper to taste

PREPARATION:

1. Sauté the bacon or pancetta and drain the oil off.

2. Add onions and garlic and sauté over a low flame for three minutes. Add carrots and cook 8 minutes longer. Add tomatoes and cook 6 minutes.

3. Add water, chicken broth, and lentils.

4. Bring to boil. Lower heat and simmer until the Lentils are tender. Tender yet a little firm, about 35 - 40 minutes.

5. Serve in soup bowls as is or you can add a little short pasta to each bowl. Drizzle extra virgin olive oil on top and pass around the Grated Parmigiano.

NOTES on The LENTIL SOUP

As stated earlier, you can make this soup with Sausages and it makes quite the hearty meal, and one any Italian will just love (the Sausages). If using sausages, you can omit the bacon or pancetta or leave it in as well. Either way is fine. Also, if you want to make this soup vegetarian, you can leave out any meat and replace the chicken stock with water or vegetable broth.

Another way to mix it up with this fine soup is to put in a bunch of escarole to the base soup. Wash the escarole, cut it into chunks and throw it in at the 35 minute mark of the soups cooking time and "Voila," you got *Lentil & Escarole Soup*. Wow!

This soup freezes well. I usually get about 4 quart containers when making this soup. I'll freeze one container and eat the other three over the next 5 to 7 days or so. It's great to have on had to make a quick and tasty meal in just 5 minutes of reheating the soup. And what could be better than that? Basta!

VINO

We can not talk about Italian Americans and Italian-American Food and not give a nod to the "Nectar of The Gods," Vino, (wine) and Bachus the Roman God of Wine. Search out a painting of Bachus, painted by the great Italian painter Caravaggio. It's a great work of art, as is all good wine. Anyway, Vino, or Wine as we know it in English is vital to the Italian Table, and especially at a Sunday meal with Sunday Sauce, a party or any large gathering centered around food.

Growing up and having all those wonderful family meals at Aunt Helen's, Uncle Jimmy's House, but especially and most often at Aunt Fran's and Uncle Tony's House in Lodi. At our Bellino Family meals, wine was always a constant. Uncle Frank is considered by all in our family as the Head of our tribe. When it came to wine, as I've previously stated, Uncle Frank pretty much liked two wines and that was it. Uncle Frank always had a bottle of Gallo Hearty Burgundy and or Carlo Rossi Paisano on hand at any time, and always in large 3 or 5 liter bottles, the kind that had a little ring handle around the top of the bottle to put a finger through. These kind of jug wines might be scoffed at and looked down upon by many people, but they have been a staple of many an old Italian guy for years, guys like Uncle Frank. Yes, they are not the greatest wines in the world, there is no question to that, but they're not as bad as some would lead you to believe. These wines; Gallo Hearty Burgundy and Carlo Rossi Paisano are what they are, and that's good (not Great) basic table wines at a low price. They have satisfied many over the years, people like Uncle Frank, Uncle Tony and so many more. Even I who got deeply into wine, creating the first Venetian Wine Bar (Bar Cichetti) in the U.S., and as Wine Director at Barbetta for a number of years. Getting so heavily into wine, I have drunken over the years what are considered the World's Greatest and most expensive wines. I have had all the famous Bordeaux's, most of the famed Burgundy's, prestigious Californian wines, and of course all the Great Italian "Trophy Wines," and more. And many times over. And all this being said and with all I know about wine and Italian Wine, I am not above drinking wines that are "considered" amongst the most "lowly" in the Wine World. And I just said a key thing about wine there. That is, "all I know about Wine." Yes I do know a lot, and knowing a lot, I know I have a lot more to learn. But I can tell you this, and I'm not going to get very far into it, but knowing as much as I do on wine, I can tell you as far as concerns what are considered great trophy and very expensive wines, a lot of it is a "Bunch of BS," and Marketing BS at that. These wines that come on the market at $325 a bottle and up just plain are not worth the money, "It's All Marketing," and creating an image of mystery that many who are gullible enough to be drawn into and buy into all the Marketing Hog-Wash. Those charging outrageously high prices for such grossly over-priced wines will gladly take their money. Believe me, it's True! I could go on and on, but I'm not. I want to talk about Italian and Italian-American Wine, Italian Food and how the food and the wine marry together as one.

Yes, I am not above drinking Carlo Rossi Paisano and Gallo Hearty Burgundy wines, especially when I'm sitting down to meal with my Uncle Frank and Uncle Tony. They like it, so, so do I. These wines are nostalgic to me. They bring back so many memories of sitting around my Aunt Fran's table at Uncle Tony's house with Aunt Helen, mommy, Jimmy, sister Barbara, brother Michael, cousin Tony, all my family and loved ones, and Carlo Rossi and Ernest and Julio Gallo were usually there too, bastions of Italian America and thee Italian American lifestyle. And if you were eating Meatballs that Aunt Helen made, Uncle Tony's Marsala, a Sunday Sauce, or Aunt Fran's Eggplant Parmigiano, you had it made.

Sometimes we might go a little upscale with a bottle of Ruffino Chianti and in later years when my cousin Tony and I got into wine, we might bring a good bottle of Chianti, Brunello, or Barolo to the table. But we never did mind drinking a glass of Carlo Rossi or Gallo Hearty Burgundy, especially with a marvelous Sunday Sauce on the table; Meatballs, Sausages, Braciole, Raviolis, and all of the foods we loved.

So anyway, after all that, let me tell you what to drink. Yes, you can have Carlo Rossi or Gallo Wine. "It's OK!" By the way, I love drinking it with my Uncles and when they offer it, but I don't buy it myself. Being in the wine business for many years, I usually don't have to buy too much wine. When I do buy wine and when I'm eating Italian Food, I always buy Italian Wine. I don't particularly care for Californian Wines that much, other than my Uncle's California jugs. If someone has it at the table, and there's nothing else, I'll drink it, but I'm not that crazy about them. Most Californian wines that Americans drink are way too thick and heavy, and clash with food and don't go well with Italian Food. But if that's what you like, go right ahead.

In Italy, most of the wines they drink have a lighter body. They are full of flavor, but are of a lesser weight, less heavy, not concentrated, thick, and manipulated. The big thick wines (California, Australia) are generally very rich and clash with food. In Italy and all over Europe, you usually drink local wines wherever you may be. The local wines go best with the local foods, every Italian and European knows that.

If you are in Tuscany, most likely you are going to drink a local wine that is probably a Sangiovese based wine, like; Chianti, or maybe Morellino, Vino Nobile, and or if you can afford it, a bottle of Brunello. All these wines go well with the local Tuscan foods. In fact, all these wines go well with most any Italian-American and Italian food in Italy, no-matter the region your in. My favorite wine when having a Sunday Sauce, Fettuccine Bolognese, Spaghetti and Meatballs, Sausage & Peppers, or whatever I'm eating, I love a good Chianti. A good Chianti, made mostly from the marvelous Tuscan Grape Sangiovese, with a bit of other local grape varietals like; Cannaiolo, Colorino, or Malvasia Nero are perfect for most any Italian dish you might be eating. Chianti should be light to medium in body with good flavor of Cherry, Sour Cherry, and a little touch of spice. One of my favorite Chianti's to drink is from Quercetto which comes from the beautiful town of Greve in the heart of Chianti Classico. In most years this wine is just right, being of light to medium body, with the previously mentioned flavor profile. I also love Chianti from; Gabbiano, Monsanto, and my friend Luigi Capellini at Castello Verrazano or another friend (Friends) at Villa Calcinaia in Greve, the brothers; Conti Sebastiano Capponi and brother Conti Niccolo Capponi.

Other wines that will go well with your meal, are; Barbera, Nebbiolo d'Alba, Barolo, Valpolicella, Aglianico, Montepulciano di Abruzzo, or Cerasaulo di Vittoria from Sicily. Oh, Whites? Yes I almost forgot about whites, and don't think I don't like them. If you want a good white wine from Italy, go for a nice Verdicchio from the Marche (Villa Buci is great), Greco di Tufo from Campania, a nice Soave (Veneto), or Gavi and Arneis from Piedmont. ,

In closing on wine, as far as Italian-Americans go as concerns wine, which wines Italian-Americans like with there meal and what they buy runs the gamut from the simple inexpensive California Jug-Wines that my uncles and many old-school Italians like, to serious Italian Wine collectors who like all the big expensive trophy wines of Italy and everything in-between. Just remember, you don't have to spend a lot of money to get a good wine. That Quercetto Chianti I mentioned usually cost just $7.99 - $8.99 the bottle, it's great, I love it, and highly recommend it. Drink what you like, even if it is an overly concentrated California or Australian Cabernet, if that's what you like. I myself will always take a good Italian wine I like, most likely; Chianti or Cerasaulo di Vittoria, or if I have the cash, a good Barolo or Brunello di Montalcino. Basta!

"In Vino Veritas"
"In Wine there is Truth"

ESPRESSO

Espresso, the making, consuming and enjoyment of a properly made Espresso is another facet and time honored tradition of Italian-Americans and their culture. We do love our properly pulled Espresso. A properly pulled Espresso is a thing of beauty and refinement, and must be done just so. We can and do make Espresso in our homes with either a Neapolitan or Moka brewing device, and now these days, there are any number of expensive new-fangled home espresso makers, more on that later.

Some might be surprised but the great art of the perfect Italian Espresso has been around for just about 110 years. Yes Italians drank Espresso before that, but it was only developed into a "Fine Art" that it is today, just a little more then a hundred years ago or so when Luigi Bezzera developed the first Espresso Machine that we know today. After this landmark in Espresso history, the consumption and popularity of Espresso grew rapidly. Caffes and Espresso Bars popped up everywhere all over Italy. These Espresso Bars were places to have an Espresso and socialize. And in Italy, there is a whole act and ritual to going to an Espresso Bar for your habitual morning coffee. And it's not just for the Espresso but some socializing, a bit of chit-chat, gossip, political talk, sports (Soccer/Futbol), this-that-and-every-other-thing. This morning Espresso is quite ritualistic in Italy, and is practiced by most, and in every corner of the country, on every other street corner in cities like; Rome, Bologna, Palermo, Milano, Verona, all over. And it is quite the sight to see, especially if you're an American going for the first time. In caffes and bars in Italy it is at the stand-up Espresso bar where all the action takes place. When you go into a caffe (a.k.a. Bar) in Italy and have a Espresso, Cappuccino, whatever, and sit at a table, that Espresso will cost you an additional 50% or more than it will if you consume it standing up at the counter at the Espresso Bar. It's a tax thing. The caffe owners are taxed on their tables and this tax gets passed on to the customer. Basta!

Anyway, the ritual of the early morning Italian Espresso? People get dressed, leave their homes and are on their way to work, but they don't go right from their house to their job. No they have to have an Espresso and the ritual of the Espresso and some Chit-Chat (BS) with a quick stop at their favorite local caffe. They might leave their house then go to an Espresso Bar near their home before going to their job, or they may head to their job, then get an Espresso at a favored caffe near the work-place. They might even do both, get an Espresso in their neighborhood before heading to work, then stopping at an Espresso Bar close to their workplace before bopping into work.

Well, that's the way they do it in Italy, quite a ritual and amazing to see. In America, Italian immigrants to cities like New York, Boston, Providence, and Philadelphia opened Social Clubs that served Espresso, maybe some sandwiches, soup, soda, Biscotti, and Anisette Toast, and Cannoli that they bought from a nearby baker. These Social

Clubs which sprung up in neighborhoods like the Lower East Side of New York or what is now called Little Italy, in Boston's North End, and San Francisco's North Beach. These Social Clubs (Caffe) were primarily of and for the working class, and were for Italians. The clubs were for Italians, and people of other nationalities did not go into them unless they were brought in by an Italian guy from the neighborhood. And that's the way it was back then.

Espresso e Dolce at home? When I was growing up and went to my Aunt Fran and Uncle Tony's house in Lodi, or to Aunt Helen's for Sunday Dinner, and we ate our meal, and it moved on to coffee and dessert, this was quite a sight that brings back nice memories for me to this very day. And it was a wonderful ritual, and unlike the quick grab your Espresso, Chit-Chat for a few minutes and run out the door as is done at caffe's and Espresso Bars in Italy, the Espresso was anything but Espresso (Fast) at Bellino Family meals, as is with millions of Italian-American families over the years. No, this was no quick hit-and-run affair. The coffee and dessert course at our family gatherings was the longest portion of our all day affair of the Sunday Meal. My Aunts and Uncles would sit around the table, we (the Kids) would too, but we would go back and forth, cause this sit-down at the table usually lasted about 3 hours, maybe more. We'd sit down, and Aunt Fran and Aunt Helen had the Neapolitan going with Espresso. The table was laden with all sorts of goodies; Cannolis of course, one or two different cakes, and an assortment of Italian

Cookies and Pastries (Sfogiatelle, Mille Foglie). There was always enough to fill Pastry Shop Showcase, "I kid you not!"

The table full of my aunts and uncles was a wonder. They'd sit around drinking coffee, eating pastries, and talk-talk-talk, about politics, sports, gossip, this-that-and-everything. My uncle Frank who was the Ring-Leader could have solved all the Worlds problems, right there at that table, filled with Cannoli, Biscotti, Coffee (Espresso), cakes, Anisette, heated discussion, laughter, and a "Bundle of Joy," all over Espresso.

Aunt Helen and Aunt Fran made the Espresso in Neapolitan Espresso Maker. The Neapolitan is from Napoli, Italy. It was developed so Neapolitans (and all Italians) could make Espresso in their homes. The Neapolitan is a two-piece device whereby, you fill the bottom of the vessel with water, the ground espresso goes in the middle and you screw on the empty top. To make Espresso with the Neapolitan you put the device on the stove over a flame with the piece filled with the water on the stove. The water heats, and when it comes to the boil, you turn the flame off, flip the vessel over so the hot water is at the top and will then drip down through the ground coffee to make the Espresso. The Espresso is not as good as that you'd get at a caffe or Espresso Bar with a large machine, but it's good enough, and adding a little shot of Anisette is never a bad thing, something my Uncle Frank always did. This is called a Caffe Corretto, the act of adding a few drops of your desire liquor into your espresso. You can add; Grappa, Sambucca, Brandy, Anisette, or other liquor to make a caffe corretto. At Aunt Fran & Uncle Tony's, it was always Anisette. Basta.

As a child it was always something to see, watching Aunt Fran or Aunt Helen go through the pleasant little ritual of making Espresso in that curious looking contraption, the Neapolitan. As I said, it always intrigued me, and when I took my first trip to Italy and was in Napoli walking through a street market and spotted a merchant selling *Neapolitans* and other kitchenware's, I just had to get myself one, a Neapolitan of my own and from the great city it was invented in, Napoli. I also brought back some beautiful ceramic plates from nearby Vietro sul Mare on the nearby Amalfi coast, and I've been making Espresso with my Neapolitan (bought in Napoli), and eating Spaghetti on those beautiful Amalfi Coast Plates from ever since, a joy, and a way to bring Italy into your own American home. Doing so, brings back beautiful memories of; Positano, The Amalfi Coast, Sicily, and the rest of Italy. If you can't be there (which is a shame), then bring Italy into your home. And that is what we do, every time we sit down to a meal, a glass of wine, or a simple little cup of Espresso, "we bring Italy home."

Sunday Sauce

DOLCE

Dolce e Dolci? Sweets! Italian Desserts; Cannoli, Gelato, Cakes, Sfogliatelle, and Cookies are among the tastiest in the World. During our family's massive Sunday Meals, of Antipasto, Maccheroni, and Sunday Sauce, the dessert course was the biggest and longest part of the meal.

After the antipasto, the pasta and the Sunday Sauce Gravy, we would sit down for dessert. The selection of sweets (dolci) and coffee (espresso & American) was mind bogglingly grand. Most times my aunts Fran and Helen would make some tasty treats. Aunt Fran made the best Ricotta Cookies ever. I used to eat them by the dozen. Aunt Helen would make, either Almond or Sesame Cookies or a Cheesecake, and in addition to these, there were always more cookies, Cannoli, Éclairs, and Sfogliatelle from the local Italian Bakery. Yes the spread was massive, and whatever wasn't consumed during the 3 hour dessert course, was divided up and given to anyone who wanted to take some sweets home. I never refused.

A three-hour dessert course? Yes, once everyone made it to dessert, the grown-ups would sit around for hours, sipping Espresso and Anisette, eating their favorite desserts and chit-chatting about this-and-that, "everything." And boy could they talk. And after eating a nice antipasto, followed by the famed Sunday Gravy, or some sort of Beef or Veal Roast with vegetables and preceded by a soup, Pasta &

Peas, or Pasta Ceci, or maybe some Raviolis, the food was rather bountiful.

I have fond memories of these days and listening to Uncle Frank, Uncle Tony, and the aunts talking about all sorts of things. When I was young, I would play with my cousins, brothers and sister. The boys and girls would usually break off into separate groups; we'd play as the grown-ups talked. I'd always drift back and forth to the table to get some more sweets and listen to a bit of the conversation, and as I got older, I'd stay longer and longer at the table, "La Tavola," spend time with the elders, the desserts, and all the fine stories of family, friends, Italy, Food, "This-That-And Every-Other-Thing." That table was always wonderful, like a magnet, always drawing me back.

ITALIANS and THEIR DESSERTS

As we've learned in the previous chapter, Italian-Americans and their desserts, when friends and family get together for family meals, the dessert can be on a massive scale. Our Italian brethren in Italy on the other hand normally are not quite as extravagant as their Italian-American cousins here in America. Often Italian (in Italy) meals at home and in restaurants end with fruit as the final course and not sweets. When Italians have dinner at home, yes it's possible they might have some sweets, but often it's some tasty fresh seasonal fruit like; a big bowl of Cherries in the middle of the table, some Watermelon, Apricots (Albicocca) or other fruit. Often Italian families will eat dinner at home without dessert, but after the meal they'll go to a caffe or pastry shop for sweets, or more often to a Gelateria for Gelato. This is the norm of many Italians and their home-cooked meals. It's savory at home then they go out for sweets to break up the night. On the other hand, they may do as we do, make something, or before hand, someone will stop at a Gelateria for Gelato to bring home to eat after dinner, or if not gelato, then some pastries or other sweets. That's the way it goes, "That's Italian."

Note: I have not included a lot of recipes for sweets in this book, just 1 in fact. This book, Sunday Sauce is dedicated more to the savory foods. I have cooked many meals for friends and families over the years. It's usually a good amount of work and time consuming. I have made desserts for people over the years here-and-there, but not that often. Like I said, it's a good deal of work and takes time, which I don't mind, I love to cook it in fact, "truly." But, when it comes to the food and desserts, I'd rather put the time into the savory food and buy dessert, or we usually have someone pick up some nice desserts for our meal, and it always works out fine. You can do whatever you like, make desserts or not. You can buy some dessert, but I usually find that since I supply the savory food, someone usually feels like bringing the "Sweets" or a bottle of wine. Don't get me wrong. I love sweets, and especially when having a little dinner party, which though it would still be great without, it would still feel like something was missing. We love our sweets, the desserts and dessert course are a wonderful component of any meal, which keeps the party going, and we "Gild-The-Lilly," so to speak. Do as you like, we almost always have dessert, *"La Dolce Vita"* (The Sweet Life).

RICOTTA CHEESECAKE

INGREDIENTS:

2 lbs. whole milk Ricotta
6 extra large Eggs
¾ cup Sugar
zest of 1 Lemon and 1 Orange (optional)
1/8 teaspoon of Salt
1 teaspoon Vanilla Extract
4 tablespoons flour
1-2 cup plain breadcrumbs & 2 tablespoons Sugar
Butter (to grease pan)

1. Grease a spring-form pan with butter. Mix bread-crumbs and 2 tablespoons of sugar together. Place mixture in buttered pan. Move breadcrumb mixture around to coat pan with mixture.

2. Beat eggs with ¾ cup of sugar. Add vanilla, and Lemon & Orange Zest if using. Add flour and continue beating ingredients together. Little by little, add the Ricotta to bowl and mix until all the ricotta is incorporated and smooth.

3. Heat oven to 375 degrees.

4. Place the spring-form pan inside a large pan. Pour all of the Ricotta (Cheesecake) mixture inside the spring-form pan. Pour warm water into the larger pan that is holding the spring-form pan with the ricotta mixture. Pour water half way up the sides of the spring-form pan. This is a water-bath.

5. Bake for 15 minute at 370 degrees. Turn oven down to 325 degree and bake cheesecake for 50 to 60 minutes more, until when you put a toothpick into the center of the cake, it comes out clean.

6. Cool cheesecake for 1 hour outside at room temperature. Place cheesecake in refrigerator and cook for 2 to 3 hours before serving.

THE NEGRONI

The Negroni? A question? A question to some, to most of America? Yes, probably. Many so-called sophisticates have been drinking this "The Negroni" quite a bit in the past 4 years or so. The truly sophisticated, worldly folks have known about them far longer. Me? I've been drinking this great Italian-Cocktail for some 28 years now. Yes, I've been drinking Negroni's ever since my first at a Bar in la Bella Roma back in the Summer of 1985. Rome, "The Eternal City" is where I had my first, on that marvelous first trip to Bella Italia. I was quite a young man, and that trip was completely magical, discovering real Italian "Italian Food" for the very first time, I had my first true Bolognese, Spaghetti Carbonara, Coda di Vacinara, Bucatini Amatriciana, Gelato, and a true Italian Espresso, "Oh Bliss!" Yes it was. I saw The Sistine Chapel, Michelangelo's Moses at San Pietro en Vincole (Saint Peter in Chains), I saw the Coliseum, The Roman Forum, The Duomo in Florence, Venice and The Grand Canal, Positano, Capri, Napoli, and so much more. Yes the trip was magical. It was magical hanging out at a Bar in the Piazza Popolo drinking my first Campari, and that first of a thousand Negroni's, or more. Many American's are just discov-ering its charms, *"me and the Negroni,"* we go way back; in Rome, Venice, Capri, Positano, Capri, Verona, Bologna, I've had Negroni's all over. And many in New York in restaurants and bars all over

Manhattan, and Staten Island where I drink some of the best Negroni's I've ever had, certainly in New York, at my buddy Pat Parotta's house in Staten Island. Pat pours an awesome Negroni, better than any bartender in the city. He makes them with love and when I go to one of his wonderful little dinner parties, that's the first thing I have. It's tradition for us now. Leaving my house in Greenwich Village, I hop on the 1 Train and take it down to the Battery to the Staten Island Ferry Terminal. I hop on the ferry, ride across New York Harbor, passing the gorgeous Lady Liberty (The Statue of Liberty) along the way. I get off the ferry. Pat picks me up at the terminal on the Staten Island side. We go to house, and I'm not through the door two minutes and he's mixing up a nice one. A Negroni that is! Well 2 that is, one for me, and a Negroni for himself. We drink great Italian Wine at those dinner parties, and some of Pat's tasty food. But we always start it off with our *ritualistic* Negroni's alla Patty "P" and you should too.

NEGRONI

Basic Recipe:

1 ounce Campari
1 ounce Sweet Vermouth
1 ounce Gin
Ice
Orange

1. Fill a Rocks-Glass or Highball Glass with Ice.

2. Add Campari, Sweet Vermouth, and Gin.

3. Stir ingredients. Garnish with a piece of Orange Peel or slice of Orange.

Note: Orsen Wells after discovering the Negroni while writing a screenplay in Rome, wrote in a correspon-dence back home that he had discovered a delightful Italian Cocktail, "The Negroni." Welles stated, *"It is made of Bitter Campari which is good for the liver, and of Gin which is bad. The two balance each other out."*

THE BELLINO NEGRONI

For me, this is the Perfect Negroni. The basic Negroni recipe calls for 3 equal parts(1 oz.) each of Camapari, Sweet Vermouth, and Gin in a glass filled with ice, and garnished with an Orange Peel.

For the most *perfectly* balanced Negroni, I put in slightly less Campari (3/4 oz.), ¾ ounce of Gin, a little more Sweet Vermouth with 1 ¼ ounces, over Ice, add a tiny splash of Club Soda and Garnish with a good size piece of Orange. Voila! The Perfect Negroni. Enjoy!

Daniel Bellino-Zwicke

Sunday Sauce

The AMERICANO

The Americano Cocktail is the older brother to the Negroni. It was created in 1860 at Caffe Camparino. The drink was first known as a Milano-Turino as the Campari came from Milano (Milan) and the Cinzno Sweet Vermouth was from Turin. The cocktail became the Americano when Italian Bartenders noticed how popular it was with American tourists. The Americano is made of 1 ½ ounces of Campari and 1 ½ ounces of Sweet Vermouth over ice, topped with a splash of Club Soda and garnished with a lemon peel.

The Americano's younger brother, the Negroni was created in 1919 at Caffe Casoni in Florence when the Count Negroni was in the caffe and wanted a drink that was a bit stronger than his usual Americano Cocktail. The Count asked the bartender to substitute Gin for the Club Soda, the Negroni was created and the rest is cocktail history.

So make a Americano, a Negroni, Campari & Soda, or a tasty Campari & Orange Juice, savor it, relax, and all will be well, "you've got Campari."

PS .. "Bond, *James Bond*." Bond drank the *Americano* in Ian Flemmings first Bond book. Agent 007 drank an Americano in "*Casino Royale*," as well as in from *A View To a Kill.*

Sunday Sauce

Daniel Bellino-Zwicke

Mangai Bene !!!

BASTA !!!!

ITALIAN FAVORITES

NEW YORK:

Bar Pitti .. One of NY's best Italian Restaurants …
270 Sixth Avenue, Greenwich Village, NY, NY

Ferdinanda's .. Best place to get a Vesteddi Sandwich
Panelle, and other Sicilian Specialties in New York ..
151 Union Street, Brooklyn, New York

Totonno's .. "Best Pizza" in New York .. Since 1926
1524 Neptune Avenue, Coney Island, Brooklyn, NY

DiFara Pizza .. "New York's Other Best Pizza, it's a
toss-up between the two?" 1424 Ave. "J" Brooklyn ..

Rocco's Patiscceria "Best Italian Pastries in NY"
243 Bleecker Street, Greenwich Village, NY

Caffe Dante … "Best Italian Caffe in New York"
79-81 Mcdougal Street, Greenwich Village, NY

Faicco's Italian Specialties "Best Italian Pork Store in
New York" Bleecker Street, Greenwich Village, NY

DiPalo's .. Great Italian Cheeses and Salumi ..
200 Grande Street, Little Italy, New York, NY

Caffe Reggio .. Historic Old Caffe with great art
works and a Renaisance Bench from a Medici Palace.
Macdougal Street, Greenwich Village, NY NY

Porto Rico Coffee .. Best Coffee by the pound in NY.
Yes they're Italian! Bleecker Street, NY NY

ITALY

Positano .. Most Beautiful Beach-Town in Italy. This beautiful little town on the Medeteranean is nestle in a large natural amphitheater with lovely homes and hotels stacked one-over-the-other. A little tow that has 2 of the world's top rated hotels and lovely seafood restaurants. Lay on the beach go swimming and savor the beauty of this beautifl peace of paradise.

Venice .. Harry's Bar, Wine Bars (Bacari), Piazza San Marco, Doges Palace, Florian's Caffe, and the entire city. It's gorgeous and a wonder of the world.

Rome .. The Roman Forum is a must see, as well as the Piazza Navona, Trattorias, The Fountains, Markets, The Sistine Chapel &Vatican, San Peitro in Vincoli, and the entire Ancient City. It's wonderous.

Verona .. The Bottega del Vino (Italy's most famous Wine Bar), The Roman Arena, and all the fine Osterias, caffes, and restaurants.

Florence .. (Firenze) The Duomo, Uffizzi Galleries, Michelangelo's statue of David, the Trattorias, especially one called Pandemonio, "it's awesome!"

Chianti Classico .. If you can, make a trip to Chianti Classico the wine region just south of Florence, it's beautiful and amazing and well worth the time.

Sicily .. Taormino, Gelato, Vino, Vesteddi, Caponata, Ancient Ruins, and Italy's best pastrries.

Castelo Verrazzano .. Greve in Chianti. One of the most beautiful wine estates in all of Italy and it's geared towards tourists. Take the tour of their cellars followed by a wonderful multi course lunch in the castle, eating local dishes with Verrazzano wines. It's a experience not to be missed.

The Leaning Tower of Pisa .. You gotta see it! I was going from Cinque Terre to Florence and jumped off the train for 2 hours just to see it. It's gorgeous.
Napoli .. A wonderful Italian city that's full of life. Napoli is the World Capital of Pizza, go there and eat some, then move on to; Capri, Sorrento, and Positano. Visit Pompei if you have the time.

Italy, anywhere and everywhere it's great, "The Most Beautiful of Beauty, The World's Tastiest Food, and Marvelous Wine, it's Italy! You can't go Wrong?"

Note: The Italian Riviera, with towns like; Portifino, Santa Margherita, and the 5 towns of Cinque Terre are quite lovely, I've been there twice. Though I must say, if you've never been to either, and you are trying to choose between the two, pick the Amalfi Coast with the capitvatingly beautiful towns of; Positano, Amalfi, Ravello, Ischia, and The Isle of Capri with Sorrento and the lively city of Naples (Napoli) nearby. If you have time, you can go to the town of Vietro Sule Mare and buy some beautiful ceramics in this little town famous for its ceramics, they are lovely, and will make your meals at home in the U.S. have a great Italian feel to them, bringing back memories of the Amalfi Coast and all of Italy.

Sunday Sauce

By The Same Author

La TAVOLA
ITALIAN-AMERICAN NEW YORKERS ADVENTURES
of The TABLE

THE FEAST of THE 7 FISH
Italian Christmas

SEGRETO ITALIANO
Secret Recipes & Favorite Dishes

GOT ANY KAHLUA?
The Collected Recipes of The Dude

Sunday Sauce

Made in the USA
Middletown, DE
20 February 2016